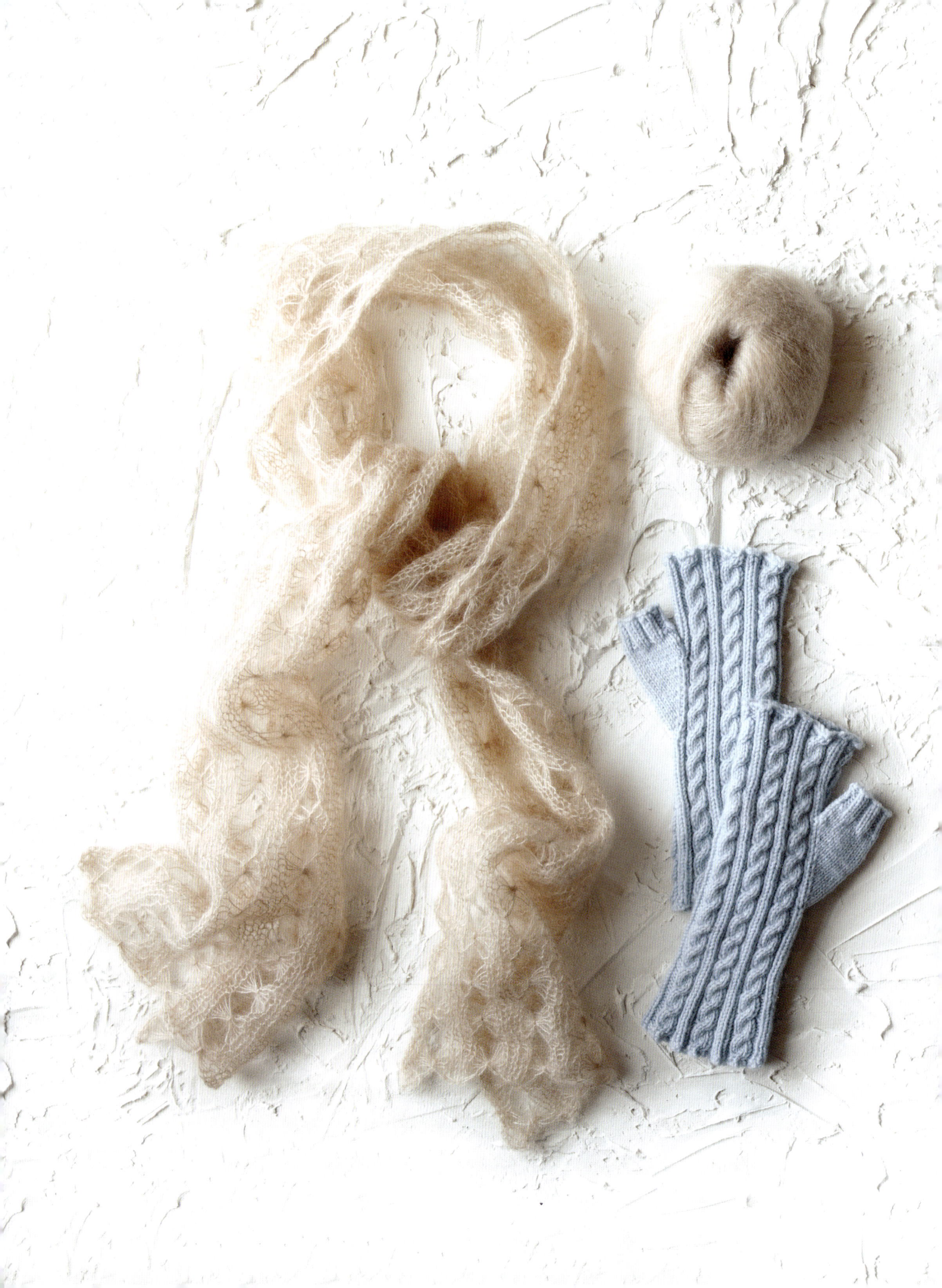

Under 100

KNIT COLLECTION
by Knit Picks

30 stashbusting projects that use under 100 grams of yarn

Copyright 2015 © Knit Picks

All rights reserved. This book or any portion thereof may not be reproduced or used in any manner whatsoever without the express written permission of the publisher except for the use of brief quotations in a book review.

Printed in the United States of America

Second Printing, 2015

ISBN 978-1-62767-029-6

Versa Press, Inc
800-447-7829
www.versapress.com

CONTENTS

INTRODUCTION 7

ACCESSORIES
Felted Tablet Cozies 10
Little Chunky Bag 14
Pikabu Boot Toppers 16
Pixie Purses 18
Twisted Lines Boot Toppers 20

COWLS
Autumn Splenor Cowl 24
Cables and Ribs Cowl 26
Diamond Cowl 28
Diamond Kerchief Cowl 30
Peaks and Valleys Cowl 34
Revesby Cowl 36
Tamalane Cowl 38
Thistledown Cowl 40

HANDS & FEET
Candy Stripes Fingerless Mitts 44
Frida Fingerless Mitts 48
Helical Socks 50
Helyx Fingerless Mitts 52
Scrunchy Ombre Arm Warmers 56
Selbu Tulip Mittens 58

HATS
Agamenticus Hat 64
Cherry Blossom Headband 66
Color Harmony Cap 68
Honey Wine Beanie 72
Nutkin 76
Rock 78

NECKWEAR
Butterfly Stitch Scarf 82
Cirruncinus Shawl 84
Fern Shawlette 88
Iona Double Ruffle Scarf 90
Silvretta Crescent Shawl 92

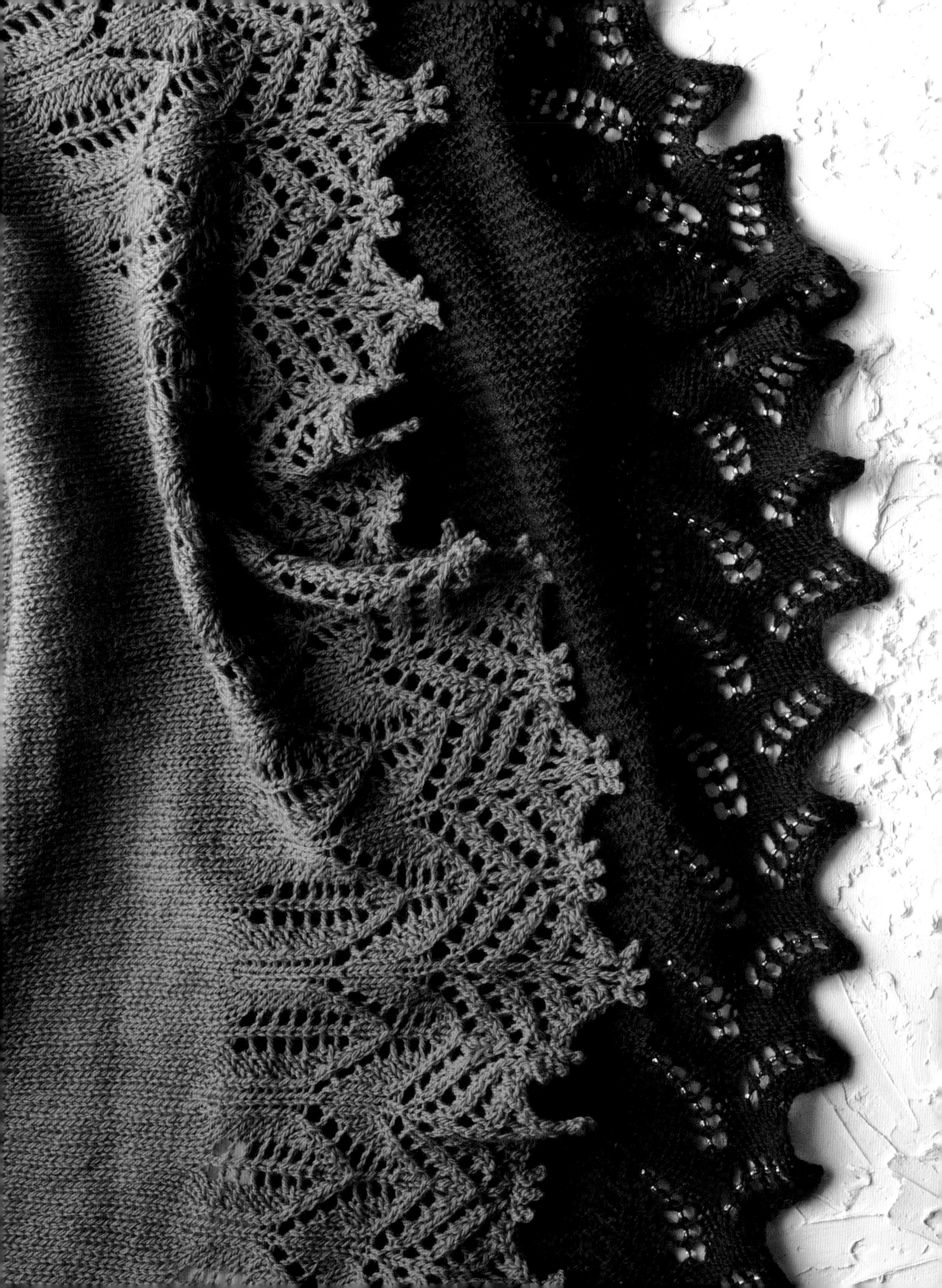

Introduction

Why is it so wonderful to finish a book in a single sitting?

It could be the instant sense of completion—or perhaps it's the magic of entering a world that's fully revealed in short order (as though you'd found a secret portal behind the wardrobe or looking glass).

This is the charm we hope to capture in our *Under 100 Knit Collection*: Projects that require less than 100 grams of yarn, but do more than just stashbust. These are projects that delight, entertain, challenge and ultimately reveal their form in just a single weekend (or afternoon, if you're really on top of your game!).

But of course, a short story needn't be plain. Whether the ordered beauty of garter stitch or the rich complexity of entwining cablework, the 30 patterns of *Under 100* represent a modern aesthetic that's informed by tradition—yielding results that are timeless, useful and infinitely giftable.

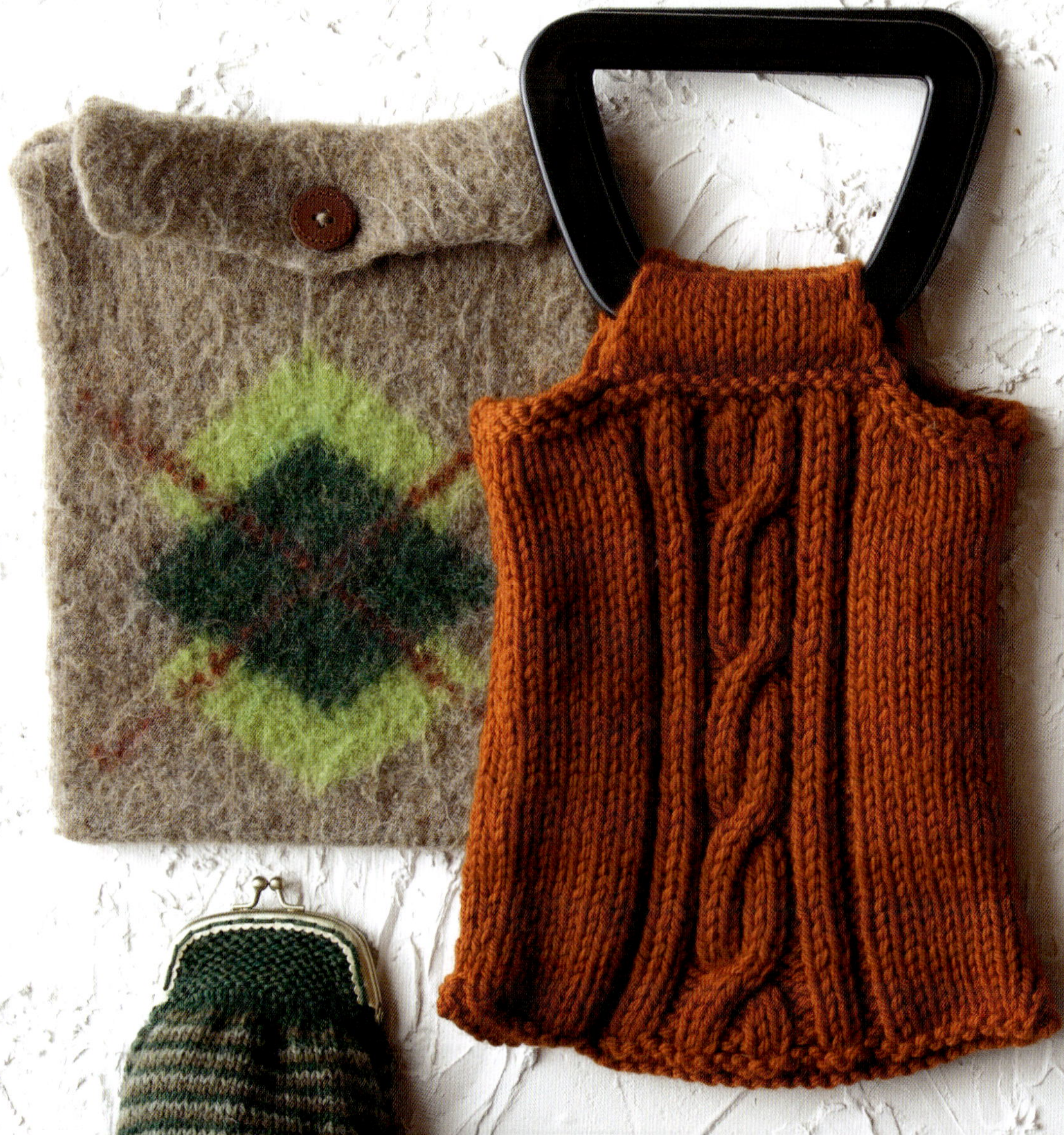

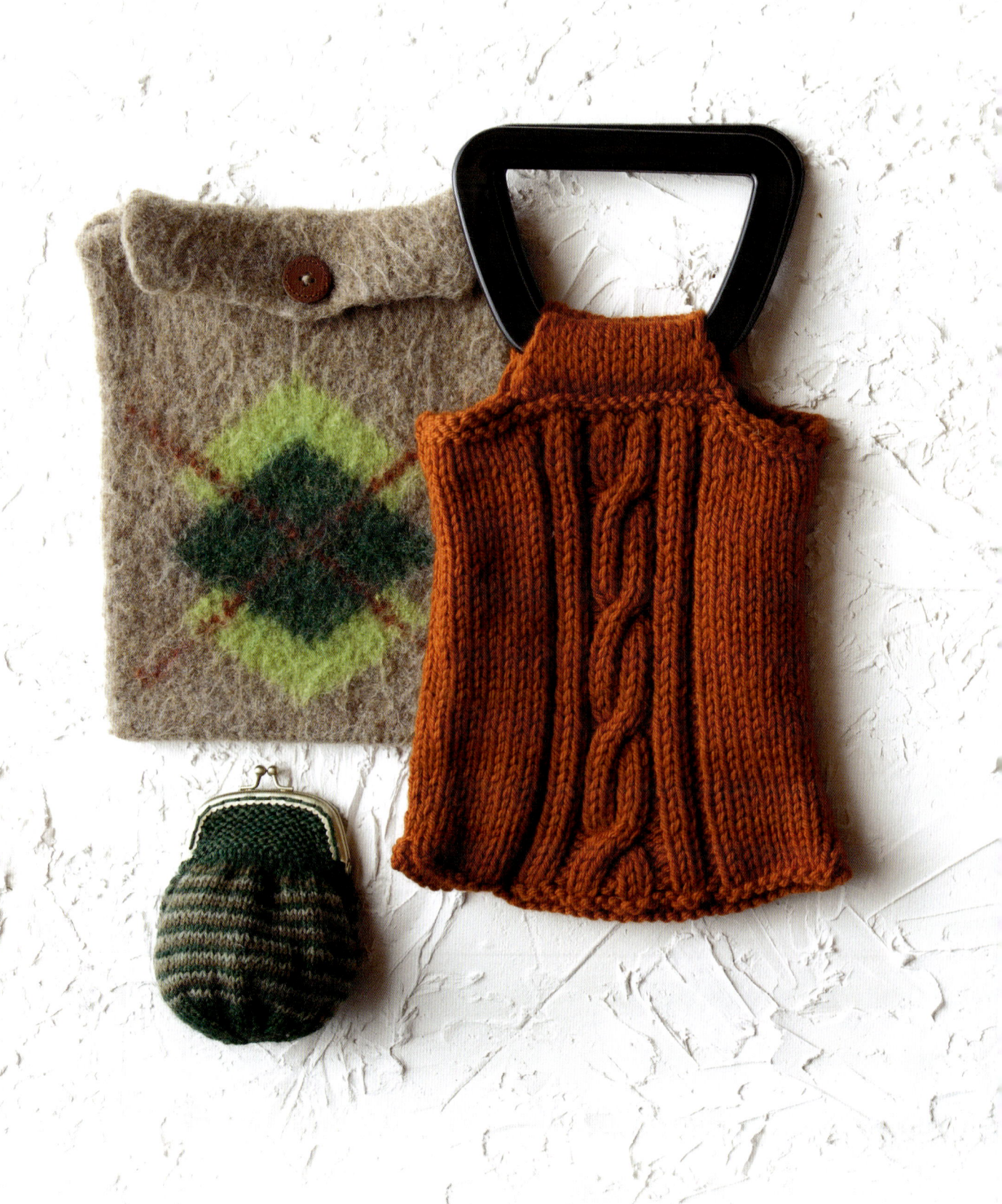

Accessories

FELTED TABLET COZIES

by Rosalyn Jung

FINISHED MEASUREMENTS
Larger tablet version: 7.75"w x 10"h
Smaller tablet version: 5.75"w x 8.75"h
Includes approximately 0.5" of ease horizontally and vertically

YARN
Larger tablet version: Knit Picks Wool of the Andes Worsted (100% Peruvian Highland Wool; 110 yds/50g)
Smaller tablet version: Knit Picks Wool of the Andes Sport (100% Peruvian Highland Wool; 137 yds/50g)

See colorwork charts for suggested colorways. You will need 1 ball of the background color, less than 1 ball of the main ground color, and a few yards of each accent color.

NEEDLES
Larger tablet version: US 10.5 (6.5mm), or size to obtain pre-felting gauge
Smaller tablet version: US 8 (5mm), or size to obtain pre-felting gauge

NOTIONS
Yarn Needle
Stitch Markers
1 flat button, ¾" diameter

GAUGE
Worsted, before felting: 14 sts/18 rows = 4" on US 10.5 needles in St st.
Sport, before felting: 16 sts and 22 rows = 4" on US 8 needles in St st
In both yarn weights, a 4" square felted down to a 3" square. Individual stitches and columns are no longer discernible.

For pattern support, contact KnitSewPretty@gmail.com

Felted Tablet Cozies

Notes:
Felted cozies for larger and smaller sized tablets in a choice of 3 intarsia designs will protect without adding much weight or thickness. Each intarsia motif is fully charted.

Numerical instructions are given for the larger size, followed by the smaller size in parentheses. Final custom sizing for similarly sized tablets can be achieved through careful monitoring of the felting process.

Cozy is worked flat in 2 pieces from the bottom up and sewn together at the sides and bottom.

All cozies are worked in stockinette stitch. The intarsia motifs are worked on both front and back pieces.

How to measure gauge:
Using one of the minor accent colors, knit a 6" swatch in pre-felting gauge. Loosely outline a 4" square with cotton yarn. Felt the swatch as described in "Finishing". Check felting progress frequently and stop when post-felting gauge is achieved. Make note of the felting process (time, temperature, etc.) so you can duplicate it for the actual cozy.

Yarns behave differently during the felting process, so be sure to swatch and test-felt before making your cozies.

Special Stitches
"Linked method" Intarsia – For the Apple and Argyles motifs, the linked (or twisted) intarsia method is recommended. At the color change, twist the yarns around each other to avoid holes in the fabric. See http://www.knitpicks.com/wptutorials/introduction-to-intarsia/

"Woven method" Intarsia – For the Flowers motif, the woven (or stranded) intarsia method is easier than the normal linked/twisted intarsia method. At the color change, introduce the motif color and weave the background color behind, as done in stranded knitting. At the end of the motif stitches, switch back to the background color. The motif color can be cut or left there to be carried up on the next row to continue with the motif.

Duplicate Stitch – http://www.knitpicks.com/wptutorials/embroidery-how-to-do-the-duplicate-stitch/

French Knots - Insert needle from underneath, wrap yarn twice around needle, insert needle back down close to where it came out.

DIRECTIONS
Back
Using the needles indicated for your chosen size, CO 39 (33) sts with background color. Starting with a purl row, work in St st for 7 rows.

Work chosen motif chart, starting with Row 1, stitch 1, at the lower right corner.

Tips for working motifs:
Apple motif – Work the apple and leaf using the linked/twisted intarsia method. Ignore the stem and work it later in duplicate stitch.

Flowers motif – Ignore the grass and leaves and work those later in duplicate stitch. Ignore the flower centers and work those later as French Knots. Work the flowers using the woven/stranded intarsia method and the stems in the linked/twisted intarsia method.

Argyles – Work the diamonds using the linked/twisted intarsia method. Ignore the intercrossing lines and work those later in duplicate stitch.

For all motifs - When working the wrong side of the motif in intarsia, it is helpful to turn your chart 180°, that is with the sheet "head down" so that the wrong side row can be worked from right to left, same as the direction of knitting.

With background color, work until 61 (67) rows from CO or until piece measures 13.5 (11.5)" from cast on edge, ending with a WS row.

Flap
Row 1 (RS): K2, ssk, k to last 4 sts, k2tog, k2 – 37 (31) sts.
Row 2: K2, p to last 2 sts, k2

Rep Rows 1 – 2 for 3 (2) more times, or until 31 (27) sts rem.

Buttonhole Row (RS): K2, ssk, k to 1 st before the middle st, BO 3 sts, k to last 4 sts, k2tog, k2.
Next Row (WS): K2, p to the bound off sts, turn work, CO 3 sts using the knitted method, turn work, p to last 2 sts, k2 – 29 (25) sts.

Rep Rows 1 – 2 until 21 (17) sts rem.

Bind off all sts.

Front
Note: Unlike the back, the motif chart for the front starts immediately after cast on.

Using the needles indicated for your chosen size, CO 39 (33) sts with background color.

Work chosen motif chart, starting with Row 1, stitch 1, at the lower right corner.

With background color, work until 61 (67) rows from CO or until piece measures 13.5 (11.5)" from cast on edge.

Bind off all sts, leaving a tail approximately 1 yd long for seaming.

Finishing
Work duplicate stitch sections and/or French Knots for your chosen motif, as indicated.

Weave in ends.

Whip-stitch the selvages of back and front pieces together at the sides and the cast on stitches at the bottom.

Insert a piece of cotton fabric (flat, not crumpled) inside the cozy to keep the front and back from felting together.

For a top loading washing machine, set it to hot water and a short cycle. Add laundry such as denim jeans and detergent. Do NOT include towels or other items that give off lint or bleed dye. Check cozy size halfway through the wash cycle, then every 5 minutes during the rest of the cycle. When it has felted sufficiently, pull the cozy and buttonhole to shape and size. If after the wash, it is still too big, wash again with laundry but stop the wash after every 2 minutes to check the size.

For front-loading machines, set it to hot water and a short cycle. Add laundry such as denim jeans and detergent. Do NOT include towels and other items that give off lint or bleed dye. At the end of the cycle, if your cozy has felted enough, pull it to shape and size. If after the wash, it has not felted sufficiently, finish felting the cozy in the dryer set to high heat and a short cycle and include the wet jeans. Check the size every 5 minutes throughout the drying cycle. Remove from dryer when it has felted to size.

Rather than inserting your tablet inside a wet or hot cozy to check for size, use a cardboard substitute instead.

Make minor adjustment to size while the piece is still wet (or wet it thoroughly) by pulling and stretching it evenly to straighten up the edges and tidy up the motif. If necessary, use your finger to enlarge the buttonhole until it fits your button. Lay the cozy on towels in a well-ventilated area to dry completely before use.

After felting, sew button in position under the buttonhole. If desired, trim the flap of the flowers motif with a crochet picot edge.

How to adjust for other tablet sizes:

Several popular tablet brands are sized similarly. Measure your tablet and choose the larger or smaller versions of this cozy pattern. Monitor the felting process carefully to achieve a customized final fit.

Tablets that differ by an inch or more in height or width may need a small adjustment in stitches and rows. When adjusting the size of the cozy, add or subtract 4.5 (5) sts per inch in width and 6 (7) rows per inch in height. Center the motif on the front of the cozy by dividing the increases or decrease evenly at both sides and top and bottom. For example, if your tablet is 1" taller than the larger version, add 6 rows before felting, which will add approximately 1" of height after felting. Remember to center the motif. In this example, raise the motif by ½", or 3 rows, from the bottom and add ½", or 3 rows, at the top.

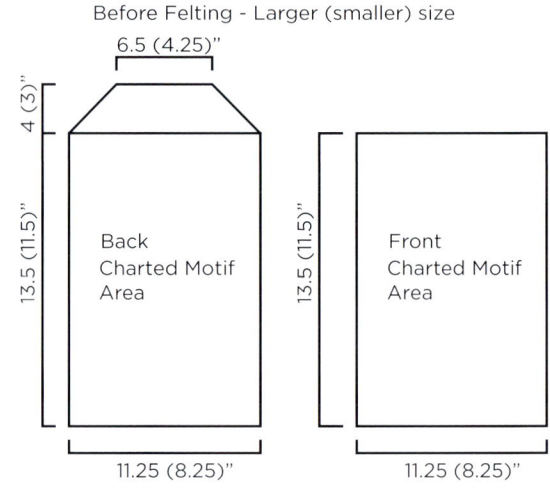

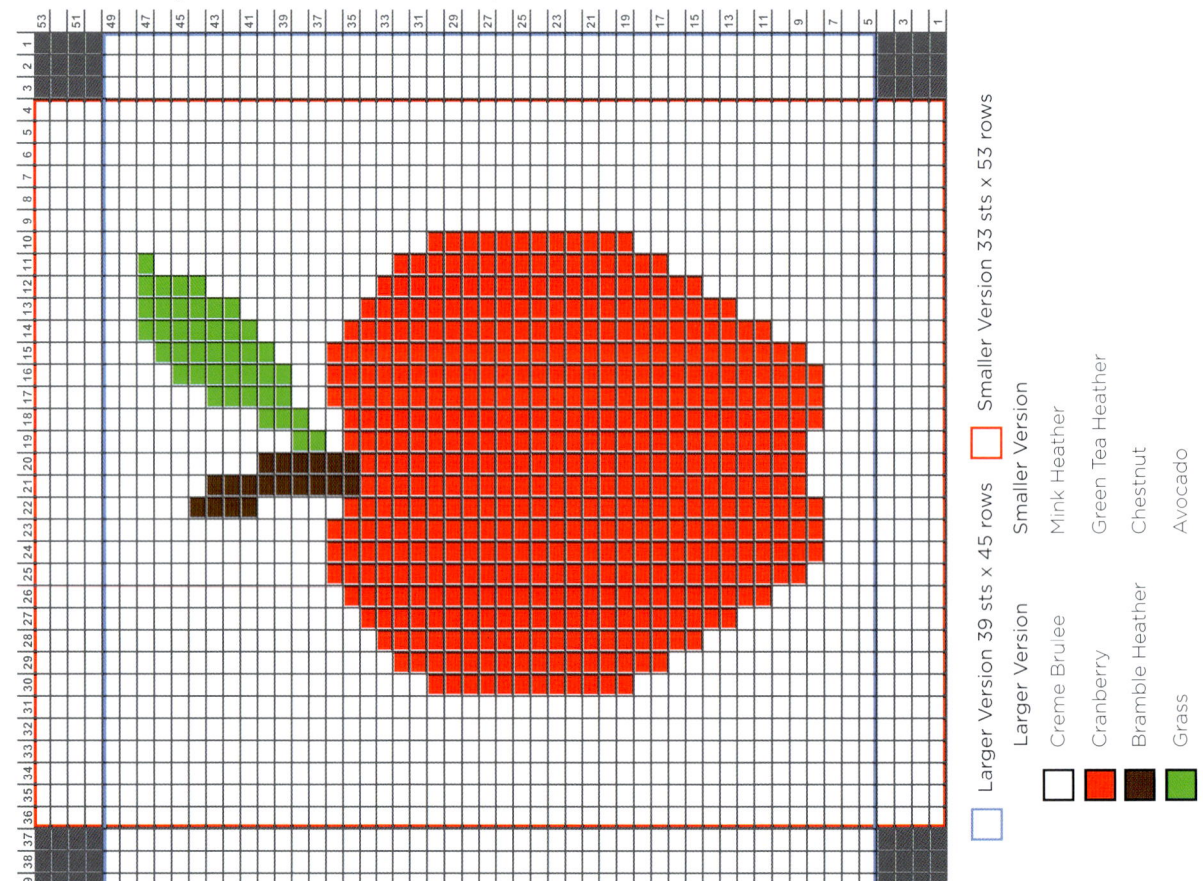

Before Felting - Larger (smaller) size

Flowers

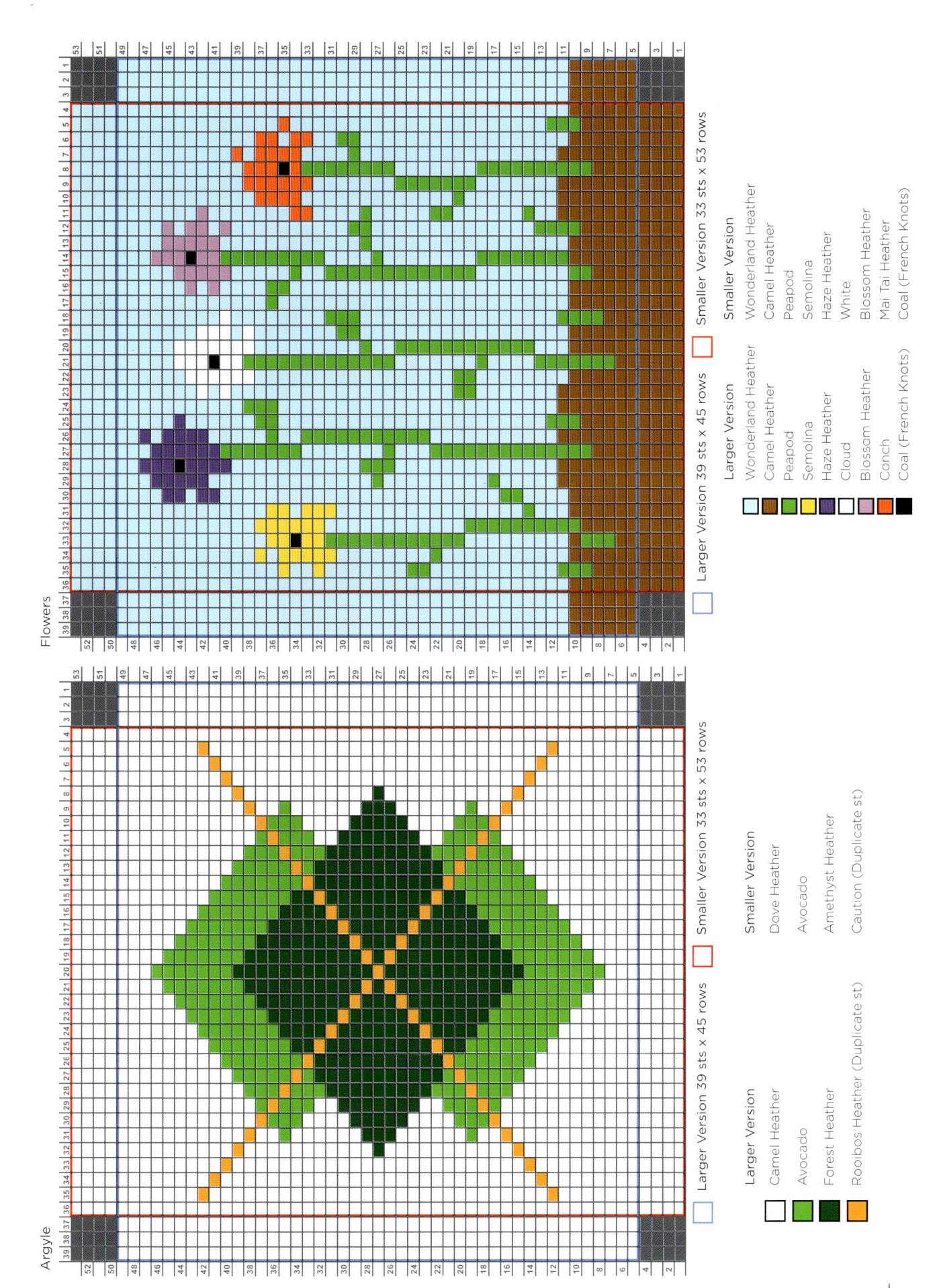

Larger Version 39 sts × 45 rows
Smaller Version 33 sts × 53 rows

Larger Version	Smaller Version
Wonderland Heather	Wonderland Heather
Camel Heather	Camel Heather
Peapod	Peapod
Semolina	Semolina
Haze Heather	Haze Heather
Cloud	White
Blossom Heather	Blossom Heather
Conch	Mai Tai Heather
Coal (French Knots)	Coal (French Knots)

Argyle

Larger Version 39 sts × 45 rows
Smaller Version 33 sts × 53 rows

Larger Version	Smaller Version
Camel Heather	Dove Heather
Avocado	Avocado
Forest Heather	Amethyst Heather
Rooibos Heather (Duplicate st)	Caution (Duplicate st)

Felted Tablet Cozies | 13

LITTLE CHUNKY BAG

by Michele DuNaier

FINISHED MEASUREMENTS
Handle width 4 (5, 6, 7, 8)"
8" or 10" in height not counting handle flap,
18" in circumference (stretches to 22")

YARN
Knit Picks Wool of the Andes Bulky (100% Peruvian Highland Wool; 137 yards/100g): Masala 24681, 1 ball

NEEDLES
US 10 (6.0 mm) knitting needles

NOTIONS
Wooden or bamboo purse handles, 4-8" wide.
Yarn Needle
Cable Needle

GAUGE
12 sts and 20 rows = 4" in St st, unblocked

For pattern support, contact mdunaier@yahoo.com

Little Chunky Bag

Notes:

Special Stitches

Cable Cross (worked over 6 sts on an RS row): Slip next 4 sts onto cable needle and hold in BACK of work, knit next 2 sts, slip 2 purl sts from cable needle to left hand needle and purl them, knit 2 sts from cable needle.

DIRECTIONS

First Handle Flap

Using size 10 knitting needles, CO 16 (18, 22, 24, 28) sts.

Row 1 (RS): K.

Row 2 (WS): P.

Row 3: K2tog, K to last 2 sts, K2tog - 14, (16, 20, 22, 26) sts.

Row 4: P.

Rows 5 – 6: Rep Rows 3 – 4 - 12, (14, 18, 20, 24) sts.

Row 7: K1, M1, K to last st, M1, K1 - 14 (16, 20, 22, 26) sts.

Row 8: P.

Rows 9 – 10: Rep Rows 7 – 8. CO 8 (7, 5, 4, 2) sts at end of Row 10 - 24 (25, 27, 28, 30) sts.

Row 11: K across. CO 8 (7, 5, 4, 2) sts at end of row - 32 sts.

Row 12: (WS): K across. (Knitting on WS of work forms a garter ridge on RS)

Row 13: K14, (K1, M1) 4 times, K14 - 36 sts.

Row 14: P9, (K2, P2) 4 times, K2, P9.

Body (Working Down the First Side)

Row 15: K9, (P2, K2) 4 times, P2, K9.

Row 16: P9, (K2, P2) 4 times, K2, P9.

Rows 17 – 18: Rep Rows 15 – 16.

Row 19: K9, P2, K2, P2, work Cable Cross over next 6 sts, P2, K2, P2, K9.

Row 20: Rep Row 16.

Rows 21 – 24: Rep Rows 15 – 16 twice.

Rows 25 – 44: Rep Rows 15 – 24 twice.

For larger size bag, repeat Rows 15 – 24 once more.

Base

Rows 45 – 52: K.

Body (Working Up the Second Side)

Rows 53 – 82: Rep Rows 15 – 24 three times.

For larger size bag, repeat Rows 15 – 24 once more.

Second Handle Flap

Row 83: K14, (K2tog) 4 times, K14 - 32 sts.

Row 84 (WS): K across. (Knitting on WS of work forms a garter ridge on RS)

Row 85: BO 8 (7, 5, 4, 2) sts, K to end of row - 24 (25, 27, 28, 30) sts.

Row 86: BO 8 (7, 5, 4, 2) sts, P to end of row - 16 (18, 22, 24, 28) sts.

Row 87: K2tog, K to last 2 sts, K2tog - 14 (16, 20, 22, 26) sts.

Row 88: P.

Rows 89 – 90: Rep Rows 87 – 88 - 12 (14, 18, 20, 24) sts.

Row 91: K1, M1, K to last st, M1, K1 - 14 (16, 20, 22, 26) sts.

Row 92: P.

Rows 93 – 94: Rep Rows 91 – 92 - 16 (18, 22, 24, 28) sts.

Row 95: K.

BO all remaining sts.

Finishing

Use yarn needle and yarn to stitch sides closed. Feed handle flaps through holes in handles and stitch flaps down inside to wrong side of work. Weave in ends.

PIKABU BOOT TOPPERS

by Laura Birek

FINISHED MEASUREMENTS
10.5 (12.5, 14.25, 16, 17.75, 19.5, 21.25)" calf circumference, roughly equivalent to sizes Teen/XS (S, M, L, 1X , 2X, 3X), worn with 0" of ease.

YARN
Knit Picks Wool of the Andes Sport (100% Peruvian Highland Wool; 137 yards/50g):
Thirst Heather 25960, 1 (1, 1, 2, 2, 2, 2) ball(s).

NEEDLES
US 5 (3.75mm) DPNs, or size to obtain gauge

NOTIONS
Yarn Needle
Stitch Markers

GAUGE
20 sts and 28 rows = 4" in St st flat, unblocked. (Gauge for this project is approximate)

For pattern support, contact info@laurabirek.com

Pikabu Boot Toppers

Notes:
This pattern is worked in two parts. First, the scalloped edging is worked flat to the appropriate length and sewn together to form a ring. Then the leg is picked up along the edging and knit downwards in the round. Because of this, the size of the piece is very customizable. If you are making this for yourself or someone who you have measurements for, you can start knitting this without worrying about gauge. Just knit the edging until it's the desired circumference. Then, pick up stitches evenly along the edge and make sure your final stitch count is a multiple of 6.

However, if you don't have measurements to work from, I've included some general sizes as guidelines.

Lace Rib (worked in the round, multiple of 6)
Row 1: *K3, YO, P3, repeat from *.
Row 2: *K4, P3, repeat from *.
Row 3: *K1, K2tog, YO, K1, P3, repeat from *.
Row 4: *K2tog, K2, P3, repeat from *.
Row 5: *K1, YO, K2tog, P3, repeat from *.
Row 6: *K3, P3, repeat from *.

Scalloped Edging
Row 1: Sl1, K2, YO, K2tog, K1, YO 3 times, K1.
Row 2: Sl1, (K1, P1, K1) into YOs, K3, YO, K2tog, K1. (10 sts)
Row 3: Sl1, K2, YO, K2tog, K5.
Row 4: BO 3, K3, YO, K2tog, K1. (7 sts)

Special Bind-off
It's important that the leg is bound off in a very stretchy manner or else it will be uncomfortable. I recommend "Jeny's Surprisingly Stretchy Bind Off" as published on the Knitty web site. The basic concept is to create a YO before each stitch you're binding off, in reverse (back to front) for knit stitches and normal YO (front to back) for purl stitches. To use this bind off in the 3x3 lace rib, work as follows:

Step 1 (knit st): Wrap yarn around right needle in reverse YO (back to front)
Step 2: K1
Step 3: Pass YO over K st.
Step 4: Wrap yarn around right needle in reverse YO (back to front).
Step 5: K1
Step 6: Pass K st and YO over. 1 st remains on right needle.

Repeat steps 4-6 for each K stitch. Then switch to P method:

Step 1 (purl st): Wrap yarn around right needle as a normal YO (front to back)
Step 2: P1
Step 3: Pass YO and previous st over. 1 st remains on right needle.

Repeat steps 1-3 until all P sts have been worked. Alternate every 3 sts in patt until all sts are bound off.

DIRECTIONS
Loosely CO 7 sts.

Work Rows 1-4 of Scalloped Edging 18 (21, 24, 27, 30, 33, 36) times or until edging measure 10.5 (12.5, 14.25, 16, 17.75, 19.5, 21.25)" from CO edge, lightly stretched.

BO all sts.

Cut yarn, leaving a 6" tail for seaming.

Being careful to not twist the work, seam CO and BO edges together using Mattress st, making sure to leave the pointed scallops unsewn.

Leg
Turn edging so the seam is facing inward.

Pick up 36 (42, 48, 54, 60, 66, 72) sts evenly along straight edge of Scalloped Edging, divide evenly between DPNs or circular needle and join in the round. Place marker to indicate beg of rnd. Work Lace Rib pat 5 times or continue until you've reached your desired length.

BO loosely using the special bind-off described above.

Finishing
Weave in ends. Blocking is not necessary for this pattern. Avoid overstretching after washing.

Lace Rib

Scallop

Legend:

V slip
Slip stitch as if to purl, holding yarn in back

knit
RS: knit stitch
WS: purl stitch

yo
RS: Yarn Over
WS: Yarn Over

k2tog
RS: Knit two stitches together as one stitch
WS: Purl 2 stitches together

yo 3x
Yarn Over three times

No Stitch
Placeholder - No stitch made.

purl
RS: purl stitch
WS: knit stitch

Bind Off

PIXIE PURSES

by Christina Wall

FINISHED MEASUREMENTS
Large Pixie Purse: 12" circumference, 4" high with bottom sitting flat on table top
Small Pixie Purse: 6" circumference, 3" high with bottom sitting flat on table top

YARN
Knit Picks Wool of the Andes Sport (100% Peruvian Highland Wool; 137 yards/50 grams) MC: Forest Heather 25285, CC1: Thyme 25280, CC2: Pampas Heather 25653, 1 skein each
Please note: the 3" Pixie Purse uses a total of 18.5 grams (~50 yards) of yarn, and the 1.5" Pixie Purse uses a total of 13.5 grams (~37 yards).

NEEDLES
US 2 (2.75 mm) DPNs, or 2 circular needles, or 1 long circular for Magic Loop, or size needed to obtain gauge

NOTIONS
Purse Frame: Large: 3" Metal Purse Frame; Small: 1.5" Metal Purse Frame (Resources to purchase the purse frames: JoAnn Fabrics or Etsy)
Stitch markers
Thin tapestry needle (needlepoint needle) for sewing purse frame to purse
Tapestry needle for weaving in yarn ends

GAUGE
26 sts and 48 rows = 4" in garter stitch unblocked, knit flat

For pattern support, contact christina.classiccables@gmail.com

Pixie Purses

Notes:
Each purse top is knitted separately in garter stitch. The body of the purse is then picked up along the cast on edge of both purse tops and joined in the round and knit down. Decreases then form the purse bottom. Each purse top is sewn to the purse frame using a thin tapestry needle.

DIRECTIONS
Large Pixie Purse
Purse Top (Make 2)
With MC, CO 20 sts using the long-tail cast on method.
Rows 1 – 3: K to end
Row 4: K1, ssk, k to 3 sts from end, k2tog, k1 (18 sts)
Row 5: K to end
Row 6: Rep Row 4 (16 sts)
Row 7: K to end
Row 8: Rep Row 4 (14 sts)
Row 9: K to end
Row 10: Rep Row 4 (12 sts)
Rows 11 – 13: K to end
BO knitwise.

Purse Body
Align purse tops with RS sides facing out. With MC, pick up 20 sts knitwise along the cast-on edge of the first purse top, then 20 sts from the second purse top (40 sts total). If you are using DPNs, you can divide them as follows: needle #1: 20 sts; needle #2, 10 sts; needle #3: 10 sts. If you are using magic loop or 2 circular needles, divide them equally. Join to work in the round.

Rnds 1 – 2: K to end
Rnd 3: Kfb into each st to end of rnd (80 sts)
Rnd 4: Join CC1, k to end
Rnd 5: K to end with MC
Rnd 6: Join CC2, k to end

Rep Rnds 4–6 six more times, for a total of seven repeats of the 3-color sequence.

Purse Bottom
Break off CC1 and CC2, work purse bottom with MC only.
Rnds 1-2: K to end.
Rnd 3: *ssk, k8, rep from * to end of rnd (72 sts)
Rnd 4: *ssk, k7, rep from * to end of rnd (64 sts)
Rnd 5: *ssk, k6, rep from * to end of rnd (56 sts)
Rnd 6: *ssk, k5, rep from * to end of rnd (48 sts)
Rnd 7: *ssk, k4, rep from * to end of rnd (40 sts)
Rnd 8: *ssk, k3, rep from * to end of rnd (32 sts)
Rnd 9: *ssk, k2, rep from * to end of rnd (24 sts)
Rnd 10: *ssk, k1, rep from * to end of rnd (16 sts)
Rnd 11: *ssk, rep from * to end of rnd (8 sts)

Break yarn, leaving a 6" tail. Thread tail onto a tapestry needle and thread tapestry needle through all sts. Take knitting needle out of sts and pull the sts together to close the hole. Weave in tail to inside of purse bottom.

Finishing
Using a thin tapestry needle and a strand of MC, sew each side of purse top to the inside of the corresponding metal purse frame top.
Lightly block. Enjoy!

Small Pixie Purse
Purse Top (Make 2)
With MC, CO 10 sts using the long-tail cast on method.
Rows 1 – 3: K to end
Row 4: K1, ssk, k to 3 sts from end, k2tog, k1 (8 sts)
Rows 5– 7: K to end
Row 8: Rep Row 4 (6 sts)
Row 9: K
Row 10: k2, sk2p, k2 (4 sts)
Row 11: K
Row 12: BO knitwise

Purse Body
Align purse tops with RS sides facing out. With MC, pick up 10 sts knitwise along the cast-on edge of the first purse top, then 10 sts from the second purse top (20 sts total). If you are using DPNs, you can divide them as follows: needle #1: 10 sts; needle #2, 5 sts; needle #3: 5 sts. If you are using magic loop or 2 circular needles, divide them equally. Join to work in the round.

Rnds 1 – 2: K to end
Rnd 3: Kfb into each st to end of rnd (40 sts)
Rnds 4 – 6: With MC, k to end
Rnds 7 – 9: With CC1, k to end

Rep Rnds 4–9 two more times, for a total of three repeats of the 2-color sequence.

Purse Bottom
Break off CC1, work purse bottom with MC only.
Rnd 1 – 3: K to end.
Rnd 4: *ssk, k8, rep from * to end of rnd (36 sts)
Rnd 5: *ssk, k7, rep from * to end of rnd (32 sts)
Rnd 6: *ssk, k6, rep from * to end of rnd (28 sts)
Rnd 7: *ssk, k5, rep from * to end of rnd (24 sts)
Rnd 8: *ssk, k4, rep from * to end of rnd (20 sts)
Rnd 9: *ssk, k3, rep from * to end of rnd (16 sts)
Rnd 10: *ssk, k2, rep from * to end of rnd (12 sts)
Rnd 11: *ssk, k1, rep from * to end of rnd (8 sts)
Rnd 12: *ssk, rep from * to end of rnd (4 sts)

Break yarn leaving a 6" tail. Thread tail onto a tapestry needle and thread tapestry needle through all sts. Take knitting needle out of sts and pull the sts together to close the hole. Weave in tail to inside of purse bottom.

Finishing
Using a thin tapestry needle and a strand of MC, sew each side of purse top to the inside of the corresponding metal purse frame top.
Lightly block. Enjoy!

TWISTED LINES BOOT TOPPERS

by Melinda VerMeer

FINISHED MEASUREMENTS
10 (12.5)" finished leg circumference, 6.5" length

YARN
Knit Picks Wool of the Andes Worsted (100% Peruvian Highland Wool; 110 yards/50g):
MC: Shire Heather 25988, CC: Cilantro Heather 25635, 1 ball each.

NEEDLES
US 8 (5mm) DPNs or circular needles, or size to obtain gauge
US 6 (5mm) DPNs or circular needles, or size to obtain gauge

NOTIONS
Yarn Needle
Stitch Marker
Cable needle

GAUGE
25.5 sts and 24 rows = 4" over cable pattern in the round, blocked using larger needle.

For pattern support, contact melinda.vermeer@gmail.com

Twisted Lines Boot Toppers

Notes:

These boot toppers are a quick way to add a colorful update to winter boots with two color cables. The small size is perfect for an ankle height boot while the large sized for a calf height lady's boot.

Two-Color Long Tail Cast On

Hold one strand of each color yarn together and tie together with slip knot approximately 36" from end. Place slip knot on needle. Slipknot will later be removed and should not be included in stitch count. Pick up working and tail yarn from MC and cast on 2 sts. Drop MC yarn and bring CC working and tail yarn between MC and cast on 2 sts. Rep until total number sts are cast on. Remove slip knot from needle.

Cable Stitch Patterns (worked over 8 sts)

4/4LC: Sl 4 sts (2 sts in MC and 2 sts in CC) onto cn and hold to FRONT, [MC] K2, [CC] K2. From cn, [MC] K2, [CC] K2.

4/4RC: Sl 4 sts (2 sts in MC and 2 sts in CC) onto cn and hold to BACK, [MC] K2, [CC] K2. From cn, [MC] K2, [CC] K2.

Twisted Lines Pattern (worked in the round over 16 sts and 8 rnds):

Rnd 1: (4/4LC, [MC] K2, [CC] K2, [MC] K2, [CC] K2) around.
Rnds 2 – 4: ([MC] K2, [CC] P2) around.
Rnd 5: ([MC] K2, [CC] K2, [MC] K2, [CC] K2, 4/4RC) around.
Rnds 6 – 8: ([MC] K2, [CC] P2) around.

Rep Rnds 1 – 8 for pattern.

DIRECTIONS

Top Cuff

Using a two-color long tail cast on with larger needle, CO 64 (80) sts. Place marker and join in round.

Rnd 1: ([MC] K2, [CC] P2) around.

Rep Rnd 1 5 additional times.

Body

Work 3 repeats of the Twisted Lines pattern.
Cut [CC] yarn, leaving a tail to weave in

Bottom Cuff

Switch to smaller needle.

Rnd 1 – 16: ([MC] K2, P2) around.

Bind off using Jeny's Surprisingly Stretchy Bind Off or your favorite stretchy bind off.

Finishing

Weave in ends, wash and block.

Twisted Lines

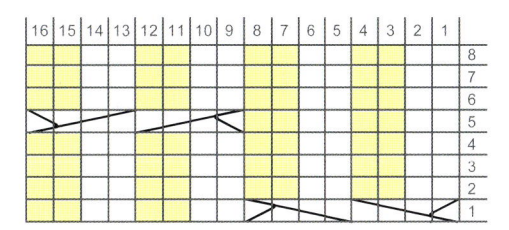

Legend:

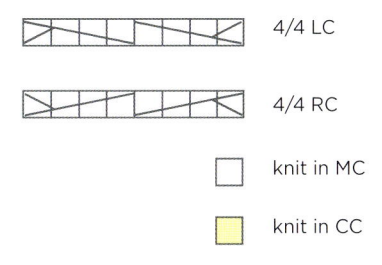

- 4/4 LC
- 4/4 RC
- knit in MC
- knit in CC

Cowls

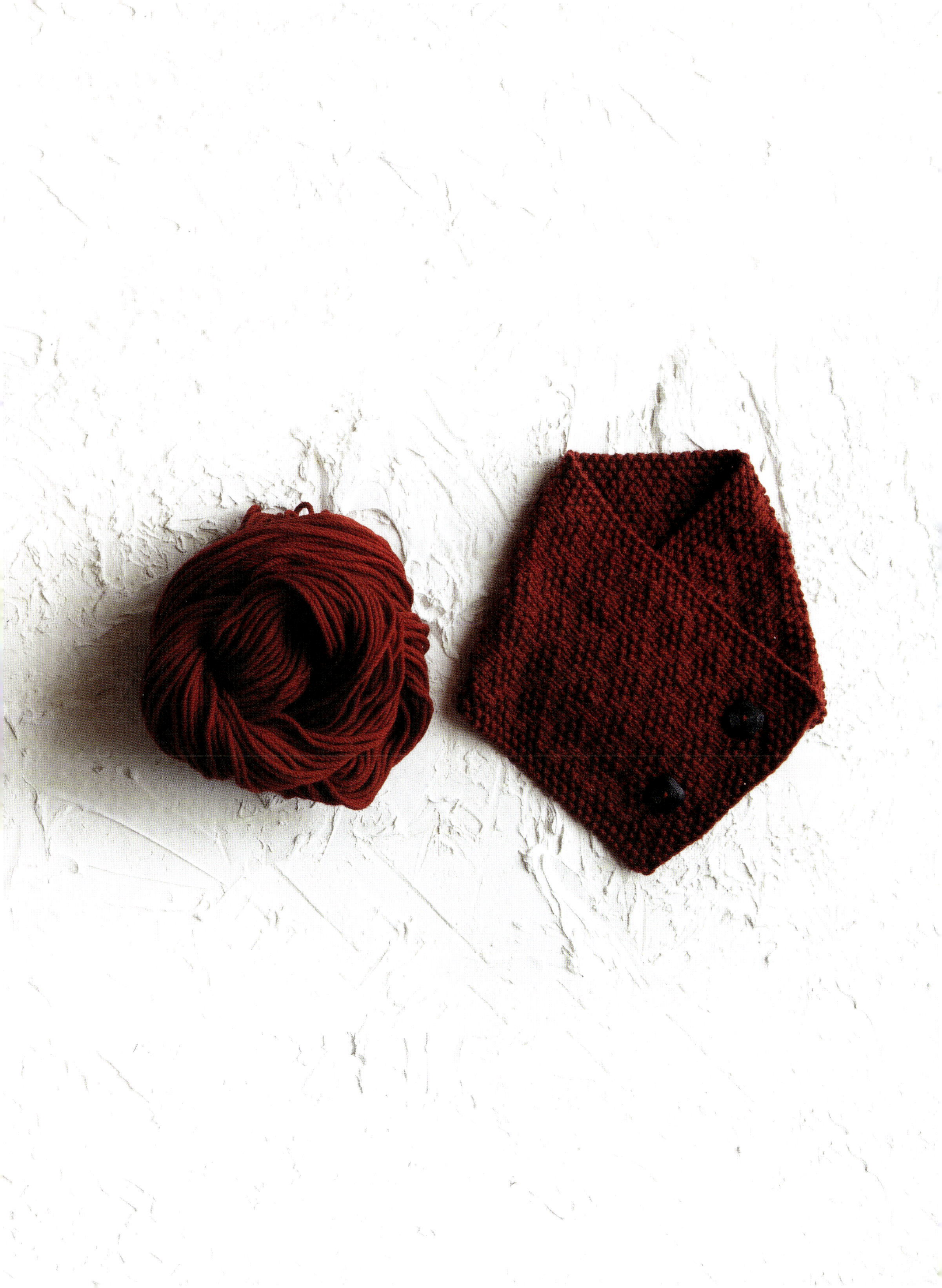

AUTUMN SPLENDOR COWL

by Jennifer Kisner

FINISHED MEASUREMENTS
5x30" Rectangle
Or
5x26"Rectangle

YARN
1 ball each of Knit Picks Wool of the Andes Worsted (100% Peruvian Highland Wool; 110yds/50g):
Color 1 – Midnight Heather 25640, 1 ball; Color 2 – Wheat 25971, Color 3 – Brass Heather 25638, Color 4 – Persimmon Heather 24280, Color 5 – Rooibos Heather 25642, Color 6 – Amber Heather 23893, Color 7 – Merlot Heather 25634, less than one ball each

NEEDLES
US 13 (9mm) straight or circular needles, or size to obtain gauge

NOTIONS
Size I or J Crochet hook or blunt-tipped tapestry needle used for seaming and weaving in ends

GAUGE
16 stitches and 15 rows = 4" in Herringbone stitch pattern with yarn doubled throughout.

For pattern support, contact thatknitchick@gmail.com

Autumn Splendor Cowl

Notes:

Autumn is a season of change. Leaves transform from their summer green to their autumn splendor. Where the bounty of the earth is harvested for the long winter ahead, and we all exchange our tank tops and cut-offs for our warm woolen mittens and thick cabled sweaters.

This pattern is perfect for the changing season. With a warm color palette that is reminiscent of the leaves of the oaks, maples & aspens, this pattern is sure to be a favorite.

It is also excellent for all those 'loose ends' you have lying around in your stash! It features the Herringbone stitch with an interesting twist. Choose 7 or even 70 colors, your choices are only limited by your imagination and stash!

Herringbone Stitch Pattern
(Worked flat) (Multiple of 2 stitches)
Row 1: S1p, K1 * S1, YO, K1, PSSO*, repeat * to * to end of row, K2
Row 2: S1p, P2tog without slipping off the left needle, P1 into the 1st stitch again, and then slip both stitches off*, repeat * to * to end of row

Special Bind-off
On WS of your last color change, *P2tog, place stitch back onto the left needle, P2tog*, repeat until there is one stitch left, cut yarn & pull the tail thru the loop.

DIRECTIONS

Cast on 22 stitches with both Color 1 and Color 2.

Row 1: With Color 1 and 2 –S1p, K1 * S1, YO, K1, PSSO*, repeat * to * to end of row, K1, SSK in the last two stitches. This only occurs on the first row of the cowl. For the rest of the pattern, row 1 ends with a K2.
Row 2: S1p, *P2tog without slipping off the left needle, P1 into the 1st stitch again, and then slip both stitches off*, repeat * to * to end of row. Break color 2.
Row 3: With Color 1 and Color 3 – Repeat Herringbone Row 1
Row 4: Repeat Herringbone Row 2. Break color 3.
Row 5: With Color 1 and Color 4 – Repeat Herringbone Row 1
Row 6: Repeat Herringbone Row 2. Break color 4
Row 7: With Color 1 and Color 5 – Repeat Herringbone Row 1
Row 8: Repeat Herringbone Row 2. Break color 5
Row 9: With Color 1 and Color 6 – Repeat Herringbone Row 1
Row 10: Repeat Herringbone Row 2. Break color 6
Row 11: With Color 1 and Color 7 – Repeat Herringbone Row 1
Row 12: Repeat Herringbone Row 2. Break color 7

Continue in the Herringbone and Color pattern. On each RS row, you will be changing colors in the color pattern. Make sure to weave in the ends of the colors while you knit. Repeat the color pattern 7 more times for a snug fitting cowl or 8 more times for a looser fitting cowl. Bind off on the WS of your last color change using the Special Bind-off.

Finishing

Weave in ends, wash and block to the dimensions listed above. Leave a long tail – about 1yrd to seam the cowl together. When seaming, attach the cast off edge to the side perpendicular or at a 90 degree angle to the cast on edge. It should make a 'V' at the bottom. Do not attach both ends together.

CABLES AND RIBS COWL

by Kimberly Voisin

FINISHED MEASUREMENTS
5" wide x 48" circumference

YARN
Knit Picks Swish Worsted (100% Superwash Merino; 110 yards/50g): Lemongrass Heather 24093, 2 balls.

NEEDLES
US 8 (5mm) straight or circular needles, or size to obtain gauge

NOTIONS
Yarn Needle
Cable needle
Spare needle
Removable Stitch Marker
Smooth waste yarn for Provisional CO

GAUGE
20 sts and 22 rows = 4" over k2,p2 rib, blocked.

For pattern support, contact kimberly_voisin@hotmail.com

Cables and Ribs Cowl

Notes:

This cowl features a series of travelling cables which move across the width of the cowl. The combination of cables and allover ribbing makes for a cowl that is both textured and stretchy. The cowl can be worn as a large loop around the neck and is long enough to wear doubled around the neck on cooler days.

Ribbing Pattern (worked flat)
Row 1 (RS): Sl1, [P2, k2] 6 times, P2, Sl1.
Row 2 (WS): P1, [K2,P2] 6 times, K2, P1.

Rep Rows 1-2 for pat.

Cable Pattern (worked flat)
Row 1 (RS): Sl1, [p2, k2] 5 times, 2/2 RC, p2, sl1.
Row 2 (WS): P1, k2, p6, [k2, p2] 4 times, k2, p1.
Row 3: Sl1, [p2, k2] 4 times, p2, 2/2 RPC, p2, k2, sl1.
Row 4: P1, [k2, p2] 6 times, k2, p1.
Row 5: Sl1, [p2, k2] 4 times, 2/2 RPC, p2, k2, p2, sl1.
Row 6: P1, k2, p2, k4, p4, [k2, p2] 3 times, k2, p1.
Row 7: Sl1, [p2, k2] 3 times, p2, 2/2 RPC, p2, 2/2 RC, p2, sl1.
Row 8: P1, k2, p4, k4, [p2, k2] 4 times, p1.
Row 9: Sl1, [p2, k2] 3 times, 2/2 RPC, p2, 2/2 RPC, k2, p2, sl1.
Row 10: P1, [k2, p2] 2 times, k4, p4, [k2, p2] 2 times, k2, p1.
Row 11: Sl1, [p2, k2] 2 times, [p2, 2/2 RPC] 2 times, p2, k2, p2, sl1.
Row 12: P1, k2, [p2, k4] 2 times, [p2, k2] 3 times, p1.
Row 13: Sl1, [p2, k2] 2 times, [2/2 RPC, p2] 2 times, 2/2 RC, p2, sl1.
Row 14: P1, k2, p4, k4, p2, k4, p4, k2, p2, k2, p1.
Row 15: Sl1, p2, k2, [p2, 2/2 RPC] 3 times, k2, p2, sl1.
Row 16: P1, [k2, p2] 2 times, [k4, p2] 2 times, k2, p2, k2, p1.
Row 17: Sl, p2, k2, [2/2 RPC, p2] 3 times, k2, p2, sl1.
Row 18: P1, k2, [p2, k4] 3 times, p4, k2, p1.
Row 19: sl1, [p2, 2/2 RPC] 3 times, p2, 2/2 RC, p2, sl1.
Row 20: p1, k2, p4, [k4, p2] 3 times, k2, p1.
Row 21: sl1, p2, k2, [p2, 2/2 RPC] 3 times, k2, p2, sl1.
Row 22: p1, k2, [p2] 2 times, [k4, p2] 2 times, k2, p2, k2, p1.
Row 23: sl1, p2, k2, [2/2 RPC, p2] 2 times, 2/2 RC, p2, k2, p2, sl1.
Row 24: p1, k2, p2, k2, p4, k4, p2, k4, p4, k2, p1.
Row 25: sl1, [p2, 2/2 RPC] 3 times, [k2, p2] 2 times, sl1.
Row 26: p1, [k2, p2] 3 times, [k4, p2] 2 times, k2, p1.
Row 27: sl1, p2, k2, p2, 2/2 RPC, p2, 2/2 RC, [p2, k2] 2 times, p2, sl1.
Row 28: p1, [k2, p2] 2 times, k2, p4, k4, [p2, k2] 2 times, p1.
Row 29: sl1, p2, k2, 2/2 RPC, p2, 2/2 RPC, [k2, p2] 3 times, sl1.
Row 30: p1, [k2, p2] 4 times, k4, p4, k2, p1.
Row 31: sl1, p2, 2/2 RPC, p2, 2/2 RC, [p2, k2] 3 times, p2, sl1.
Row 32: p1, [k2, p2] 3 times, k2, p4, k4, p2, k2, p1.
Row 33: sl1, p2, k2, p2, 2/2 RPC, [k2, p2] 4 times, sl1.
Row 34: p1, [k2, p2] 6 times, k2, p1.
Row 35: sl1, p2, k2, 2/2 RC, [p2, k2] 4 times, p2, sl1.
Row 36: p1, [k2, p2] 4 times, k2, p6, k2, p1.
Row 37: sl1, p2, 2/2 RPC, [k2, p2] 5 times, sl1.
Row 38: p1, [k2, p2] 6 times, k2, p1.

Special Stitches:
2/2 RC: Slip 2 stitches onto the cable needle and hold to the back, K2, K2 from the cable needle.

2/2 RPC: Slip 2 stitches onto the cable needle and hold to the back, K2, P2 from the cable needle.

DIRECTIONS

Note: When slipping the first and last stitch on each right side row, make sure yarn is held to the back of work.

*With waste yarn, Provisionally CO 28 sts.

Work Rows 1-2 of Ribbing Pattern 3 times.

Work Rows 1-38 of Cable Pattern from chart or written instructions.

Work Rows 1-2 of Ribbing Pattern until the cowl measures 12" from the CO edge, ending with a WS row.*

Attach a removable stitch marker at the beginning of the next row to mark the start of the next section. This marker will act as a beginning point for measure the length of the next section.

Rep instructions between * and * 3 more times, placing marker at beg of each rep to indicate start of each section.

Finishing

Carefully remove the waste yarn from the CO edge and place the live sts on a spare needle. With right sides facing outwards, graft together the two ends of the cowl using Kitchener st. After all of the stitches have been worked, weave in ends, wash and block.

Cable Chart

Legend

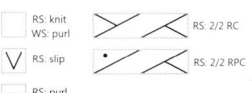

- RS: knit / WS: purl
- RS: slip
- RS: purl / WS: knit
- RS: 2/2 RC
- RS: 2/2 RPC

DIAMOND COWL

by Emily Kintigh

FINISHED MEASUREMENTS
5x21" (5x23", 7x24", 7x26")

YARN
Knit Picks Swish Bulky (100% Superwash Merino Wool; 137 yards/100g): Hollyberry 25124, 1 skein.

NEEDLES
US 10 ½ (6.5mm) straight or circular needles, or size to obtain gauge

NOTIONS
Yarn Needle
Two 1 3/8" (34mm) buttons
Thread to sew on buttons

GAUGE
16 sts and 24 rows = 4" over diamond pattern, blocked.

For pattern support, contact auntieemsstudio@gmail.com

Diamond Cowl

Notes:

The child sizes are 5 inches wide and the adult sizes are 7 inches wide. The lengths given are meant to fit snugly around necks with the circumference listed. For a looser fit or to size for a different neck circumference, simply repeat the chart more (or less) times as desired.

The seed stitch border will curl a bit when cowl is being worked, but will flatten out nicely after blocking.

Seed Stitch Bind-off
Bind-off should be worked in seed stitch pattern. Instead of knitting every stitch, alternate between knit and purl stitches beginning with a knit stitch. Otherwise, bind-off normally.

DIRECTIONS

For child sizes: CO 21 st, for adult sizes: CO 29 st.
Beginning on the wrong side:
Row 1: (K1, P1) to last st, K1.
Rows 2 and 3: Repeat row 1.

Main Cowl

Child Sizes
Repeat rows 1-8 of Diamond Pattern- Child Sizes chart 14(16) times. Cowl should measure 19(21)" from cast-on edge.

Adult Sizes
Repeat rows 1-8 of Diamond Pattern- Adult Sizes chart 16(18) times. Cowl should measure 22(24)" from cast-on edge.

Buttonholes

If adjusting for different sizes, continue pattern repeats until cowl measures 2" less than desired length. Work as follows to form the buttonholes:

Child Sizes
Rows 1 and 2: Work rows 1 and 2 of Diamond Pattern- Child Sizes chart.

Row 3: (K1, P1) twice, K1, BO next three stitches, (There should be 5 st, a buttonhole gap then 1 st on the right-hand needle.), (P1, K1) twice, BO next three stitches, (There should be 5 st, a buttonhole gap, 5 st, a second buttonhole gap, then 1 st on right-hand needle.), (P1, K1) twice.
Row 4: (K1, P1) twice, K1, CO 3 st, (K1, P1) twice, K1, CO 3 st, (K1, P1) twice, K1.
Rows 5-7: Work rows 5-7 from Diamond Pattern- Child Sizes chart.
Row 8: (K1, P1) to last st, K1.
Rows 9 and 10: Repeat row 8.

BO in seed stitch.

Adult Sizes
Row 1: K1, P1, K3, P1, K1, BO next three stitches, (There should be 7 st, a buttonhole gap then 1 st on the right-hand needle.), K2, P1, K1, P1, K3, BO next three stitches (There should be 7 st, a buttonhole gap, 9 st, a second buttonhole gap, then 1 st on right-hand needle.) P1, K3, P1, K1.
Row 2: K1, P1, K1, P3, K1, CO 3 st, K1, P3, K1, P3, K1, CO 3 st, K1, P3, K1, P1, K1.
Rows 3-7: Work rows 3-7 from Diamond Pattern- Adult Sizes chart.
Row 8: (K1, P1) to last st, K1.
Rows 9 and 10: Repeat row 8.

BO in seed stitch.

Finishing

Weave in ends, wash and block to finished measurements.

To determine button placement, first lay cowl lengthwise with wrong side up. Next, fold the end without the buttonholes over and down at an angle, then do the same to the end with buttonholes. Arrange them so that the bind off edge (with buttonholes) is lying along the side of the piece underneath. Place markers where buttons should go. Sew on buttons.

Diamond Chart - Adult Sizes

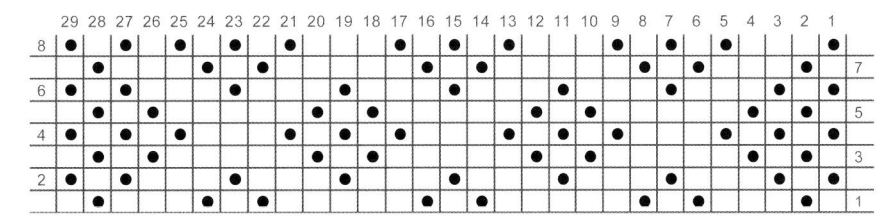

Diamond Chart - Child Sizes

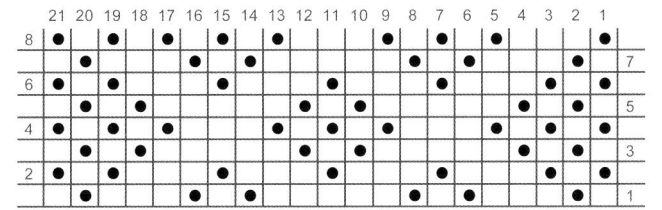

Legend:
knit
RS: knit stitch
WS: purl stitch

purl
RS: purl stitch
WS: knit stitch

Odd rows are worked on the right side and even rows are worked on the wrong side.

DIAMOND KERCHIEF COWL

by Alexis Hoy

FINISHED MEASUREMENTS
20" long from neck edge to kerchief point, 7" long at back neck, 22" circumference

YARN
Knit Picks Swish Worsted (100% Superwash Merino Wool; 110 yards/50g): Dublin 23884, 2 balls.

NEEDLES
US 7 (4.5mm) 24" circular needle, or size to obtain gauge

NOTIONS
Yarn Needle
Stitch Marker
Scrap yarn or 2 stitch holders

GAUGE
18 sts and 23 rows = 4" in St st, blocked.

For pattern support, contact herself@alexishoy.ca

Diamond Kerchief Cowl

Notes:
This cowl is knit starting with the point of the triangular front. The yarn-overs at the edges of the diamond lace pattern create the increases which build the kerchief shape. The two edges of the triangle are then joined by casting on additional stitches and working the rest of the cowl in the round. A good method for this is the knitted cast on.

Please note that gauge is extremely important. The pattern uses the full amount of yarn, and a looser gauge may result in the amount falling short.

Special Stitches
Central Double Decrease (CDD)
Slip 2 tog, K1, pass sl sts over tog.

Knit into Front and Back (KFB)
K into front and back of same stitch (inc 1)

DIRECTIONS
Kerchief Front
Note: This part of the cowl is worked flat. In the first 6 rows, a 5-stitch selvage in garter stitch is established on each side.

CO 1 stitch.
Row 1: KFB (2 sts)
Row 2: KFB twice (4 sts)
Row 3: [KFB, K1] twice (6 sts)
Row 4: KFB, K3, KFB, K1 (8sts)
Row 5: KFB, K5, KFB, K1 (10 sts)
Row 6: Knit.

Begin Diamond Lace Pattern

Note: Chart 1 shows Diamond Lace Pattern for beginning of kerchief front from row 7 through 46.

Row 7: K5 (selvage right), YO (point of first diamond), K5 (selvage left) (11 sts)
Row 8: (and all even numbered rows): K5, P all lace pattern sts, K5
Row 9: K5, YO, K1, YO, K5 (13 sts)
Row 11: K5, YO, K3, YO, K5 (15 sts)
Row 13: K5, YO, K5, YO, K5 (17sts)
Row 15: K5, YO, K7, YO K5 (19 sts)
Row 17: K5, YO, K9, YO, K5 (21 sts)
Row 19: K5, YO, K1, YO, K2tog, K5, SSK, YO, K1, YO, K5 (23 sts)
Row 21: K5, YO, K3, YO, K2tog, K3, SSK, YO, K3, YO, K5 (25 sts)
Row 23: K5, YO, K5, YO, K2tog, K1, SSK, YO, K5, YO, K5 (27 sts)
Row 25: K5, YO, K7, YO, CDD, YO, K7, YO, K5 (29 sts)
Row 27: K5, YO, K9, YO, K2tog, K8, YO, K5 (31 sts)
Row 29: K5, [YO, K1, YO, K2tog, K5, SSK] twice, YO, K1, YO, K5 (33 sts)
Row 31: K5, [YO, K3, YO, K2tog, K3, SSK] twice, YO, K3, YO, K5 (35 sts)
Row 33: K5, [YO, K5, YO, K2tog, K1, SSK] twice, [YO, K5] twice (37 sts)
Row 35: K5, [YO, K7, YO, CDD,] twice, YO, K7, YO, K5 (39 sts)
Row 37: K5, YO, K9, YO, K2tog, K7, SSK, YO, K9, YO, K5 (41 sts)
Row 39: K5, YO, K11, YO, K2tog, K5, SSK, YO, K11, YO, K5 (43 sts)
Row 41: K5, YO, K13, YO, K2tog, K3, SSK, YO, K13, YO, K5 (45 sts)
Row 43: K5, YO, K15, YO, K2tog, K1, SSK, YO, K15, YO, K5 (47 sts)
Row 45: K5, YO, K17, YO, CDD, YO, K17, YO, K5 (49 sts)
Row 47: K5, YO, K19, YO, K2tog, K18, YO, K5 (51 sts)
Row 49: K5, [YO, K1, YO, K2tog, K15, SSK] twice, YO, K1, YO, K5 (53 sts)
Row 51: K5, [YO, K3, YO, K2tog, K13, SSK] twice, YO, K3, YO, K5 (55 sts)
Row 53: K5, [YO, K5, YO, K2tog, K11, SSK] twice, [YO, K5] twice (57 sts)
Row 55: K5, [YO, K7, YO, K2tog, K9, SSK] twice, YO, K7, YO, K5 (59 sts)
Row 57: K5, [YO, K9, YO, K2tog, K7, SSK] twice, YO, K9, YO, K5 (61 sts)
Row 59: K5, [YO, K1, YO, K2tog, K5, SSK] 5 times, YO, K1, YO, K5 (63 sts)
Row 61: K5, [YO, K3, YO, K2tog, K3, SSK] 5 times, YO, K3, YO, K5 (65 sts)
Row 63: K5, [YO, K5, YO, K2tog, K1, SSK] 5 times, [YO, K5] twice (67 sts)
Row 65: K5, [YO, K7, YO, CDD] 5 times, YO, K7, YO, K5 (69 sts)
Row 67: K5, YO, K9, [YO, K2tog, K8] 5 times, YO, K5 (71 sts)
Row 69: K5, [YO, K1, YO, K2tog, K5, SSK] 6 times, YO, K1, YO, K5 (73 sts)
Row 71: K5, [YO, K3, YO, K2tog, K3, SSK] 6 times, YO, K3, YO, K5 (75 sts)
Row 73: K5, [YO, K5, YO, K2tog, K1, SSK] 6 times, [YO, K5] twice (77 sts)
Row 75: K5, [YO, K7, YO, CDD] 6 times, YO, K7, YO, K5 (79 sts)
Row 77: K5, [YO, K9, YO, K2tog, K7, SSK] 3 times, YO, K9, YO, K5 (81 sts)
Row 79: K5, [YO, K11, YO, K2tog, K5, SSK] 3 times, YO, K11, YO, K5 (83 sts)
Row 81: K5, [YO, K13, YO, K2tog, K3, SSK] 3times, YO, K13, YO, K5 (85 sts)
Row 83: K5, [YO, K15, YO, K2tog, K1, SSK] 3 times, YO, K15, YO, K5 (87 sts)
Row 85: K5, [YO, K17, YO, CDD] 3 times, YO, K17, YO, K5 (89 sts)
Row 87: K5, YO, K19, [YO, K2tog, K18] 3 times, YO, K5 (91 sts)

Transition
Note: You will now cast on a few stitches and join to work the cowl in the round. The selvage edges are placed on stitch holders to be worked later.

Row 88 (WS): K5, place these 5 stitches on holder, P to last 5 sts. K5

Row 89 (joining row): K5, place these 5 stitches on holder, [YO, K1, YO, K2tog, K15, SSK] 4 times, YO, K1.

Without turning work, CO 18 sts using the knitted cast on method, PM and join to work in the round (100 sts).

Diamond Kerchief Cowl | 31

Upper Cowl

Note: Chart 2 shows the pattern repeat for the upper cowl. The beginning stitch marker will migrate with the addition of yarn overs, as the outline indicates. This is compensated for in row 106 of the written instructions.

Rnd 90 (and all even rows from 92 - 104 & 108 - 126): Knit
Rnd 91: [YO, K3, YO, K2tog, K13, SSK] 5 times
Rnd 93: [YO, K5, YO, K2tog, K11, SSK] 5 times
Rnd 95: [YO, K7, YO, K2tog, K9, SSK] 5 times
Rnd 97: [YO, K9, YO, K2tog, K7, SSK] 5 times
Rnd 99: [YO, K1, YO, K2tog, K5, SSK] 10 times
Rnd 101: [YO, K3, YO, K2tog, K3, SSK] 10 times
Rnd 103: [YO, K5, YO, K2tog, K1, SSK] 10 times
Rnd 105: [YO, K7, YO, CDD] 10 times
Rnd 106: Knit to last stitch, Sl1, remove marker, Sl last stitch back to left needle, PM. Slipped stitch becomes first stitch of next row.
Rnd 107: [K2tog, K8, YO] 10 times
Rnd 109: [K2tog, K5, SSK, YO, K1, YO] 10 times
Rnd 111: [K2tog, K3, SSK, YO, K3, YO] 10 times
Rnd 113: [K2tog, K1, SSK, YO, K5, YO] 10 times
Rnd 115: [CDD, YO, K7, YO] 10 times
Rnd 117: [K2tog, K7, SSK, YO, K9, YO] 5 times
Rnd 119: [K2tog, K5, SSK, YO, K11, YO] 5 times
Rnd 121: [K2tog, K3, SSK, YO, K13, YO] 5 times
Rnd 123: [K2tog, K1, SSK, YO, K15, YO] 5 times
Rnd 125: [CDD, YO, K17, YO] 5 times
Rnd 127: [K2tog, K18, YO] 5 times

Ribbed Edge
Rows 128 & 129: [K1, P1] rep to end.

BO in rib.

Finishing selvage edge
Note: The selvage edge is now worked perpendicular to the edge of the back neck so that the garter stitch pattern is not interrupted.

Lay cowl flat with front side facing down.

Move stitches from holder on left side of cowl onto left needle starting with outer stitch so that stitches are set up to work a WS row.

Next Row (WS): With left needle, PU 1 st from edge of cowl. K2tog, K to end. Turn.
Next Row (RS): K4, Sl1, PU & K stitch from edge of cowl, PSSO. Turn.

Work these two rows until edging reaches its opposite side, ending with a WS row.

Using Kitchener Stitch, graft facing stitches together.

Finishing
Weave in ends, block lightly.

Chart 1

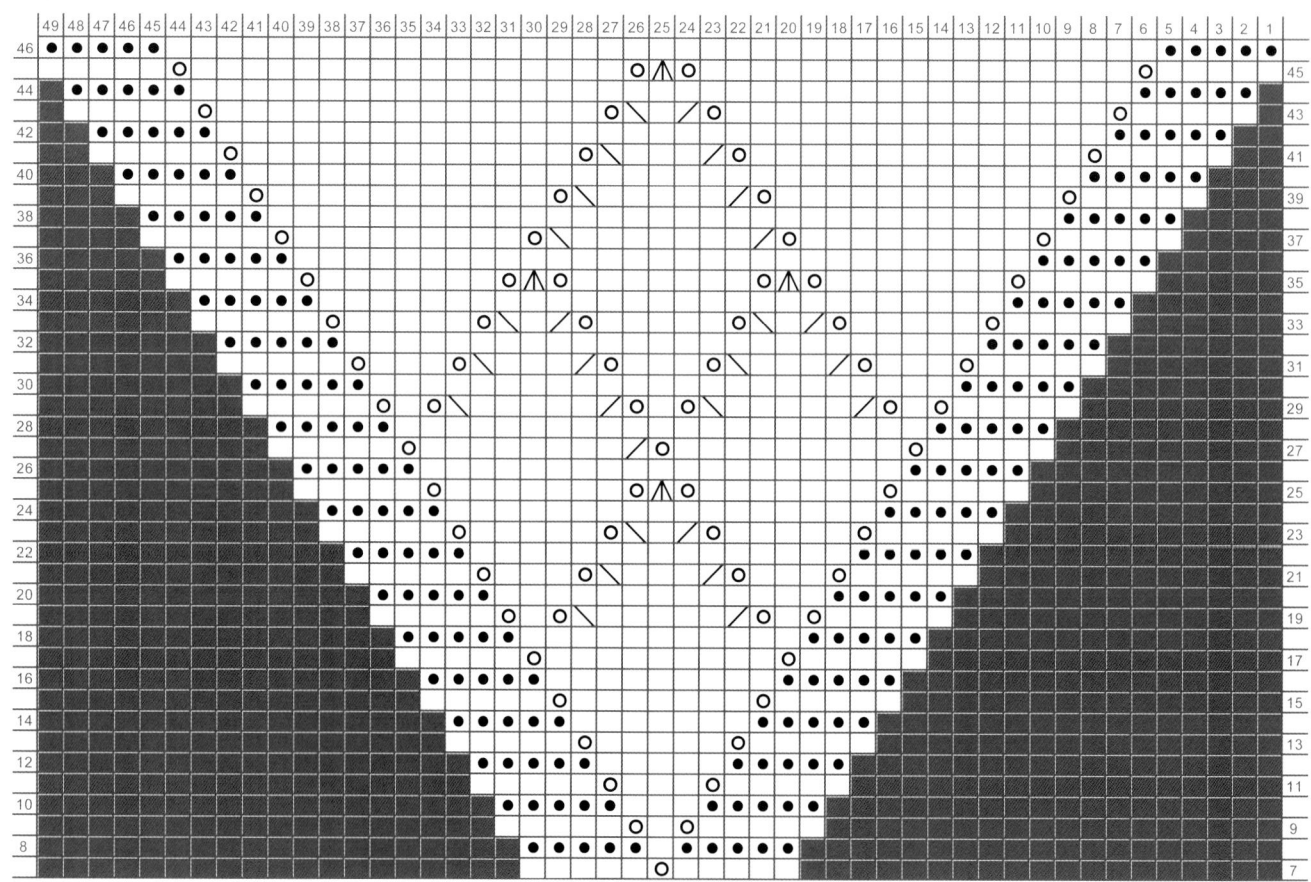

Chart 2

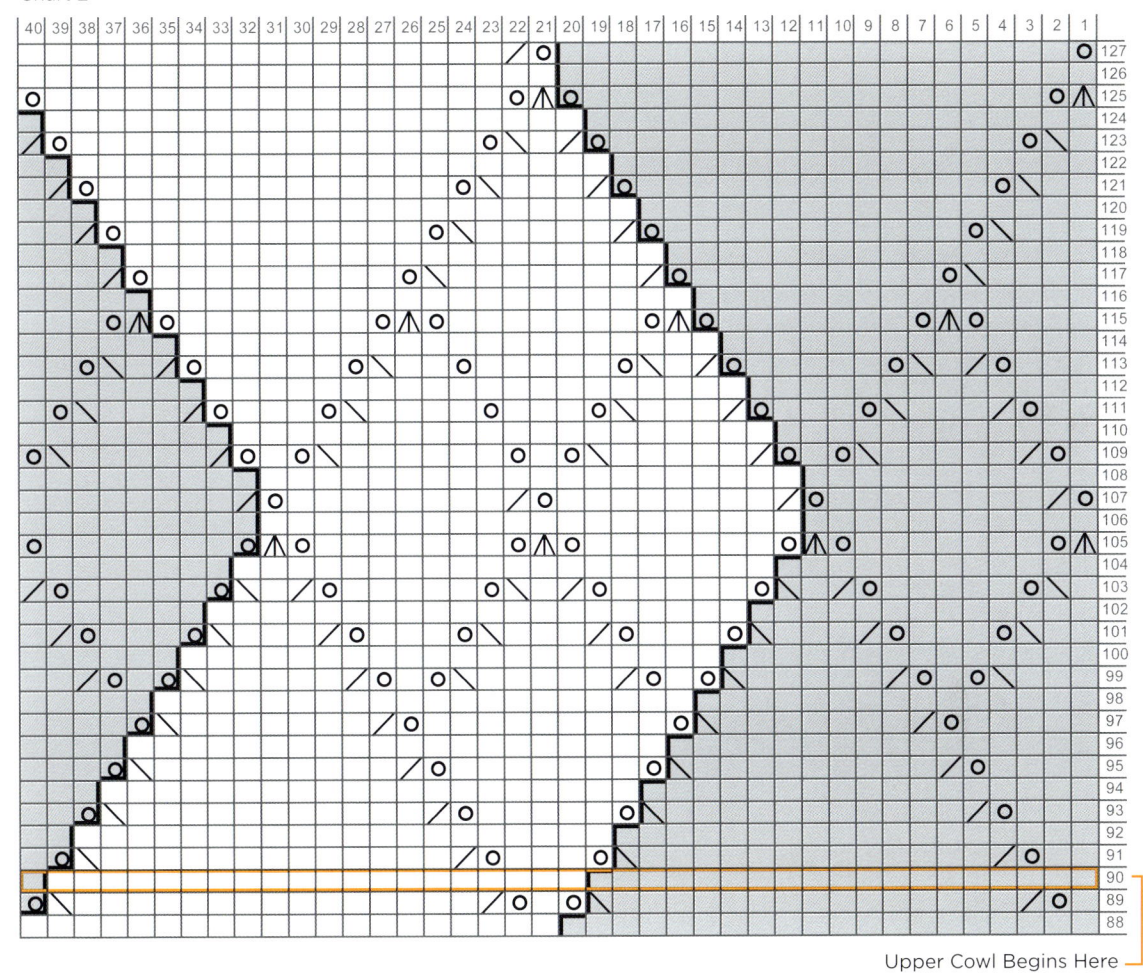

Upper Cowl Begins Here

Legend:

No Stitch
Placeholder - No stitch made.

knit
RS: knit stitch
WS: purl stitch

yo
RS: Yarn Over
WS: Yarn Over

purl
RS: purl stitch
WS: knit stitch

k2tog
RS: Knit two stitches together as one stitch
WS: Purl 2 stitches together

ssk
RS: Slip one stitch as if to knit, Slip another stitch as if to knit. Insert left-hand needle into front of these 2 stitches and knit them together
WS: Purl two stitches together in back loops, inserting needle from the left, behind and into the backs of the 2nd & 1st stitches in that order

Central Double Dec
RS: Slip first and second stitches together as if to knit. Knit 1 stitch. Pass two slipped stitches over the knit stitch.

Diamond Kerchief Cowl | 33

PEAKS AND VALLEYS COWL

by Kerin Dimeler-Laurence

FINISHED MEASUREMENTS
10" deep x 28" circumference

YARN
Knit Picks Diadem (50% Baby Alpaca, 50% Mulberry Silk; 329 yards/100g): A Smoky Quartz 26350, B Turquoise 26343, C Moonstone 26347, 30 grams each.

NEEDLES
US 2 (3 mm) straight or circular, or size to obtain gauge

NOTIONS
Tapestry Needle
Scrap yarn for provisional CO

GAUGE
28 sts and 32 ridges (64 rows) = 4" in Garter st, blocked.

For pattern support, contact customerservice@knitpicks.com

Peaks and Valleys Cowl

Notes:
Increases and decreases give a bold design to this simple, striped cowl. It is knit sideways and then grafted at the end.

CDD (Centered Double Decrease)
Slip two stitches to the RH needle as if to K2tog. Knit the next stitch, then pass two slipped sts over; two sts removed.

DIRECTIONS
Row 1 (RS): K2tog, K4, M1R, K1, M1L, K4, CDD, K4, M1R, K1, M1L, K9, CDD, K4, M1R, K1, M1L, K4, CDD, K9, M1R, K1, M1L, K4, CDD, K4, M1R, K1, M1L, K4, SSK.
Row 2: Knit.

Stripe Pattern:
Work rows 1-2 with A
Work rows 1-2 with B
Work rows 1-2 with C
Repeat these 6 rows for pattern.

With C, CO 71 sts. Knit one row; this will be a WS row.

Begin working Stripe Pattern, adding new colors as you reach them and then carrying the unused colors up the side of the work. Work in pattern until piece measures about 28" when measured along the edge. Work Stripe pattern for 5 rows. Break A and B. Break color C, leaving a 6 foot tail for grafting.

Finishing
Bring the cast on edge and the live sts together with RS showing. Using yarn tail in C, graft the live sts to the first row of sts above the CO.

Weave in ends, wash and block.

REVESBY COWL

by Brenda Castiel

FINISHED MEASUREMENTS
25" in circumference, 8" in height at widest point.

YARN
Knit Picks City Tweed DK (55% Merino Wool, 25% Superfine Alpaca, 20% Donegal Tweed; 123 yards/50g), Color A: Toad 24978, Color B: Desert Sage 24539, 1 ball each.

NEEDLES
US 5 (3.75mm) straight or circular needles, or size to obtain gauge
Spare DPN in gauge size, to work applied i-cord

NOTIONS
Yarn Needle
Stitch Markers
Waste yarn and crochet hook for optional provisional cast-on

GAUGE
22 sts and 28 rows = 4" in st st pattern, blocked.
Gauge is not critical in this pattern, but a different gauge will affect yardage and size of finished item.

For pattern support, contact bcastiel@yahoo.com

Revesby Cowl

Notes:
This attractive cowl is comprised of 2 rectangles, each bisected into two triangles. It uses intarsia to create the design. Increases and decreases keep the intarsia border straight and even. Applied i-cord provides an elegant smooth edging. There is short-row shaping so that the lower edge is wider than the top edge. Choose two pretty colors and cast on!

Short Rows:

W&T: Work to the stitch indicated. Wrap next stitch as follows: Insert right needle into the front of the next stitch purlwise, sl st onto right needle, bring yarn to front of work, sl st back to left needle; turn work, bring yarn to front (or back if purling).

Picking up wraps: When you come to the wrapped st, insert the needle into the wrap and the st to be knitted; knit together (or purl, as required).

RLI (Right lifted increase): Lift first leg of st below the next st onto needle and knit this stitch.

LLI (Left lifted increase): Lift last leg below last knitted st onto needle and knit this stitch.

Applied I-Cord:
On circular needle or DPN, cast on 4 sts. *Slide the sts to the opposite end of the ndl. K3, sl 1 purlwise. With left hand tip, pick up a stitch on edge of stole. Slip the last st on right ndl tip back onto left tip. K2tog. Repeat from * until all sts on cowl edge are worked, changing from color A to color B to match the body of the cowl.

DIRECTIONS

First Half
With Color A, CO 44 sts using long-tail cast-on or provisional cast-on.
Row 1 (WS): P to end
Row 2 (RS): K to last 4 sts, K2tog, K1, attach Color B, twist 2 colors tog as for intarsia, KFB in Color B - 44 sts (42 sts Color A, 2 sts in Color B)
Row 3 (and all WS rows until Row 85): P to end, working sts in same color as row below, twisting 2 colors tog at color change.
Row 4: K until 3 sts remain in Color A, K2tog, K1, twist, change to Color B, K1, LLI - (41 sts Color A, 3 sts in Color B)
Row 6: K until 3 sts remain in Color A, K2tog, K1, twist, change to color B, K2, LLI.
Row 8: K until 3 sts remain in Color A, K2tog, K1, twist, change to color B, K2, LLI, K1.
Row 10: K until 3 sts remain in Color A, K2tog, K1, twist, change to color B, K2, LLI, K to end.

Note: Short Rows are used to shape the cowl so that it sits nicely on the shoulders. When working these rows, you will work part way across a row (RS), turn, then work back to the beginning (WS).

Short Row 1: Work 15 sts in patt, W&T, work to end in patt
Rows 12 – 19: Rep Rows 10 – 11 four times.
Short Row 2: Work 20 sts in patt, W&T, work to end in patt.
Rows 20 – 27: Rep Rows 10 – 11 four times.
Short Row 3: Work 15 sts in patt, W&T, work to end in patt.
Rows 28 – 35: Rep Rows 10 – 11 four times.
Short Row 4: Work 20 sts in patt, W&T, work to end in patt.
Rows 36 – 43: Rep Rows 10 – 11 four times.
Short Row 5: Work 15 sts in patt, W&T, work to end in patt.
Row 44: Rep Row 10.
Rows 45 – 80: Rep Rows 9 – 10 18 times. 3 sts remain in color A.
Row 82: K2tog, K1, twist, change to Color B, K2, LLI, K to end.
Row 84: K2tog, twist, change to Color B, K2, LLI, K to end.
Row 86: With Color B, K2tog next 2 sts (1 Color B st and 1 Color A sts), K2, LLI, K to end.

Second Half:
Switch to Color A.
Row 1 (WS): P to end.
Row 2 (RS): K1 in Color B, twist 2 colors tog as for intarsia, K to end in Color A.
Row 3 (and all WS rows until Row 85): P to end, working sts in same color as row below, twisting 2 colors tog at color change.
Row 4: RLI, K1 in Color B, twist, change to Color A, K1, SSK, K to end.
Row 6: K1, RLI, K1 in Color B, twist, change to Color A, K1, SSK, K to end.
Row 8: K until 2 sts remain in Color B, RLI, K2 in Color B, twist, change to Color A, K1, SSK, K to end.
Rows 9 – 38: Rep Rows 7 – 8 15 times.

Note: When working short rows, you will work part way across a row (RS), turn, then work back to the beginning (WS).

Short Row 1: Work 15 sts in patt, W&T, work to end in patt.
Rows 40 – 47: Rep Rows 8 – 9 four times.
Short Row 2: Work 20 sts in patt, W&T, work to end in patt.
Rows 48 – 55: Rep Rows 8 – 9 four times.
Short Row 3: Work 15 sts in patt, W&T, work to end in patt.
Rows 56 – 63: Rep Rows 8 – 9 four times.
Short Row 4: Work 20 sts in patt, W&T, work to end in patt.
Rows 64 – 71: Rep Rows 8 – 9 four times.
Short Row 5: Work 15 sts in patt, W&T, work to end in patt.
Row 72: Rep Row 8.
Rows 73 – 78: Rep Rows 7 – 8.
Row 79: Rep Row 7.
Row 80: K until 2 sts remain in Color B, RLI, K2 in Color B, twist, change to Color A, K1, SSK, K2.
Row 82: K until 2 sts remain in Color B, RLI, K2 in Color B, twist, change to Color A, K1, SSK, K1.
Row 84: K until 2 sts remain in Color B, RLI, K2 in Color B, twist, change to Color A, K1, SSK.
Row 86: K until 2 sts remain in Color B, RLI, K1 in Color B, twist, change to Color A, SSK.

Break off Color B, continue working with Color A only.

Row 87 (WS): P to end.
Row 88 (RS): K to end.

Leave sts live for grafting (if you cast on provisionally), or bind off.

Graft provisional cast-on edge to live sts, or alternately sew cast-on edge to bound-off edge.

Finishing

Work applied i-cord along upper and lower edges of cowl, changing colors so that i-cord matches the color of the body of the cowl. Or alternately, use contrasting color for i-cord. Weave in ends. Block.

TAMALANE COWL

by Luise O'Neill

FINISHED MEASUREMENTS
17.75 (21, 24)" circumference x 6" high.

YARN
Knit Picks Swish Worsted (100% Superwash Merino Wool; 110 yards/50g): MC Allspice 24297, 51 (60, 68) yds; CC1 Green Tea Heather 26070, 36 (42, 48) yds, CC2 Honey 26066, 36 (42, 48) yds.

NEEDLES
US 10 (6mm) set of 5 DPNs, or one 16" circular needle, or two 24" or longer circular needles for two circulars technique, or one 32" or longer circular needle for Traveling Loop or Magic Loop technique, or size to obtain gauge
US 7 (4.5mm) one DPN or needle 3 sizes smaller than needle used to obtain gauge

NOTIONS
Yarn Needle
Stitch Marker

GAUGE
18 sts and 34 rows = 4" over stitch pattern, blocked (see Notes), using larger needles.
16 sts and 22 rows = 4" in Stockinette stitch, blocked.

For pattern support, contact patternsupport@impeccableknits.ca

Tamalane Cowl

Notes:
This reversible cowl is knit in the round using three different colors which are carried up the inside of the work, leaving minimal ends to weave in later. Always carry the working yarn under both colors not being used. This will tuck waiting yarns into the work and avoid loose strands, making the cowl reversible.

Gauge is measured over a hand-washed and air-dried swatch. Although this yarn is machine washable and dryable, to maintain the beauty of the stitch pattern in this design, hand washing and laying the cowl flat to dry is recommended.

Stitch Pattern (worked in the round over an even number of sts)
Round 1 (MC): Knit.
Round 2 (MC): Purl.
Round 3 (CC1): K1, SL 1 wyib.
Round 4 (CC1): P1, SL 1 wyib.
Round 5 (CC2): Knit.
Round 6 (CC2): Purl.
Round 7 (MC): SL 1 wyib, K1.
Round 8 (MC): SL 1 wyib, P1.
Round 9 (CC1): Knit.
Round 10 (CC1): Purl.
Round 11 (CC2): K1, SL 1 wyib.
Round 12 (CC2): P1, SL 1 wyib.
Round 13 (MC): Knit.
Round 14 (MC): Purl.
Round 15 (CC1): SL 1 wyib, K1.
Round 16 (CC1): SL 1 wyib, P1.
Round 17 (CC2): Knit.
Round 18 (CC2): Purl.
Round 19 (MC): K1, SL 1 wyib.
Round 20 (MC): P1, SL 1 wyib.
Round 21 (CC1): Knit.
Round 22 (CC1): Purl.
Round 23 (CC2): SL 1 wyib, K1.
Round 24 (CC2): SL 1 wyib, P1.

Stretchy Bind-off
The bind off for this cowl is based on Jeny's Surprisingly Stretchy Bind Off (http://www.youtube.com/watch?v=abBhe-JYmgI). It is worked in a Knit 1, Purl 1 rib to provide a wonderfully stretchy bind off. The direction in which yarn overs are created is very important - before working a knit stitch, a Yfrn is used; before working a purl stitch, a YO is used. Using a smaller needle for the bind off keeps the edge from flaring.

Jogless Bind Off in the Round
To finish the bind off round without a jog, see Jogless Bind Off (http://www.impeccableknits.ca/techniques.html#CORound) or follow these steps:

With 1 stitch remaining on RH needle, cut yarn leaving a 6" tail. Holding yarn at back of work, insert RH needle tip through 2 top loops of first bound off stitch, bring the yarn around needle as if to knit and pull yarn through all 3 loops on needle. Pull the yarn tail through rem loop.

Yfrn
bring yarn up behind the right needle, then over around the needle and to the back again between the needles to form a yarn over ready to knit the next stitch

DIRECTIONS
With larger needle(s) and MC, CO 80 (94, 108) sts. Place marker and join for working in the round, being careful not to twist sts.

Work Rnds 1-24 of Stitch Pattern 2 times, then Rnds 1-2 once more. Remove the end of round marker.

Bind Off
Using MC and smaller DPN as the RH needle, BO as follows:

Yfrn, K1, pass Yfrn over the knit stitch and off the needle, * YO, P1, pass 2 sts over (pass both the yarn over and the last stitch on RH needle over first stitch and off the needle), Yfrn, K1, pass 2 sts over; rep from * to end, ending with YO, P1, pass 2 sts over.

End this round by working the Jogless Bind Off in the Round.

Finishing
Carefully weave in ends to make this cowl reversible. Hand wash and lay flat to dry.

THISTLEDOWN COWL

by Erica Jackofsky

FINISHED MEASUREMENTS
7.5" wide x 24 (36)" wearable length, plus closure.

YARN
Knit Picks Gloss DK (70% Merino wool, 30% Silk; 123 yards/50g): Clover 25591, 2 balls.

NEEDLES
US 5 (3.75mm) straight or circular needles, or size to obtain gauge
US 7 (4.5mm) straight or circular needles, or size to obtain gauge

NOTIONS
Yarn Needle

GAUGE
22.5 sts and 19 rows = 4" over lace pattern on larger needles, blocked.
18 sts and 26 rows = 4" in stockinette on larger needles.

For pattern support, contact Erica@FiddleKnits.com

Thistledown Cowl

Notes:
The Thistledown Cowl is worked from the edge to the ribbed closure. You will begin knitting with your larger needles and then drop down two sizes to pull the stitches in for the ending. Wear this piece by wrapping the lace portion around your neck and tucking it through the ribbed loop end. Note that there is a bit of sewing required to secure the ribbing down once you've finished knitting.

Stitch count varies between right side and wrong side rows. Count stitches only after completing a wrong side row.

Lace Chevron Stitch Pattern (worked flat)
Row 1: K3, K2tog, K2, *YO, K2, SK2P, K2; rep from * to last 7 sts, YO, K2, SKP, K1, YO, SSK.
Row 2: P7, *YO, P6; rep from * to last 6 sts, YO, P4, YO, P2tog.

DIRECTIONS
Using larger needles, cast on 42 sts.

Work in lace chevron stitch pattern until piece measures 22 (34)" from beginning, or desired wearable length. (Remember that the piece will grow slightly during blocking.)

Change to smaller needle.

Knit 1 row.

Decrease Row: *P2tog; rep from * to end – 21 sts.

Purl 1 row.

Ribbing
Row 1 (WS): P1, *K1, P1; rep from * to end.
Row 2 (RS): K1, *P1, K1; rep from * to end.

Repeat these 2 rows until ribbing measures 6"

Bind off all stitches.

Finishing
Thread a tapestry needle with yarn.

Fold ribbed portion back to WS of piece and whip stitch bound off edge to the wrong side of first ribbed row. This forms the ribbed section into the looped closure. Make sure not to sew sides of ribbing so they remain open for the scarf end to be inserted.

Weave in ends, wash and gently block to 7.5" wide x desired length.

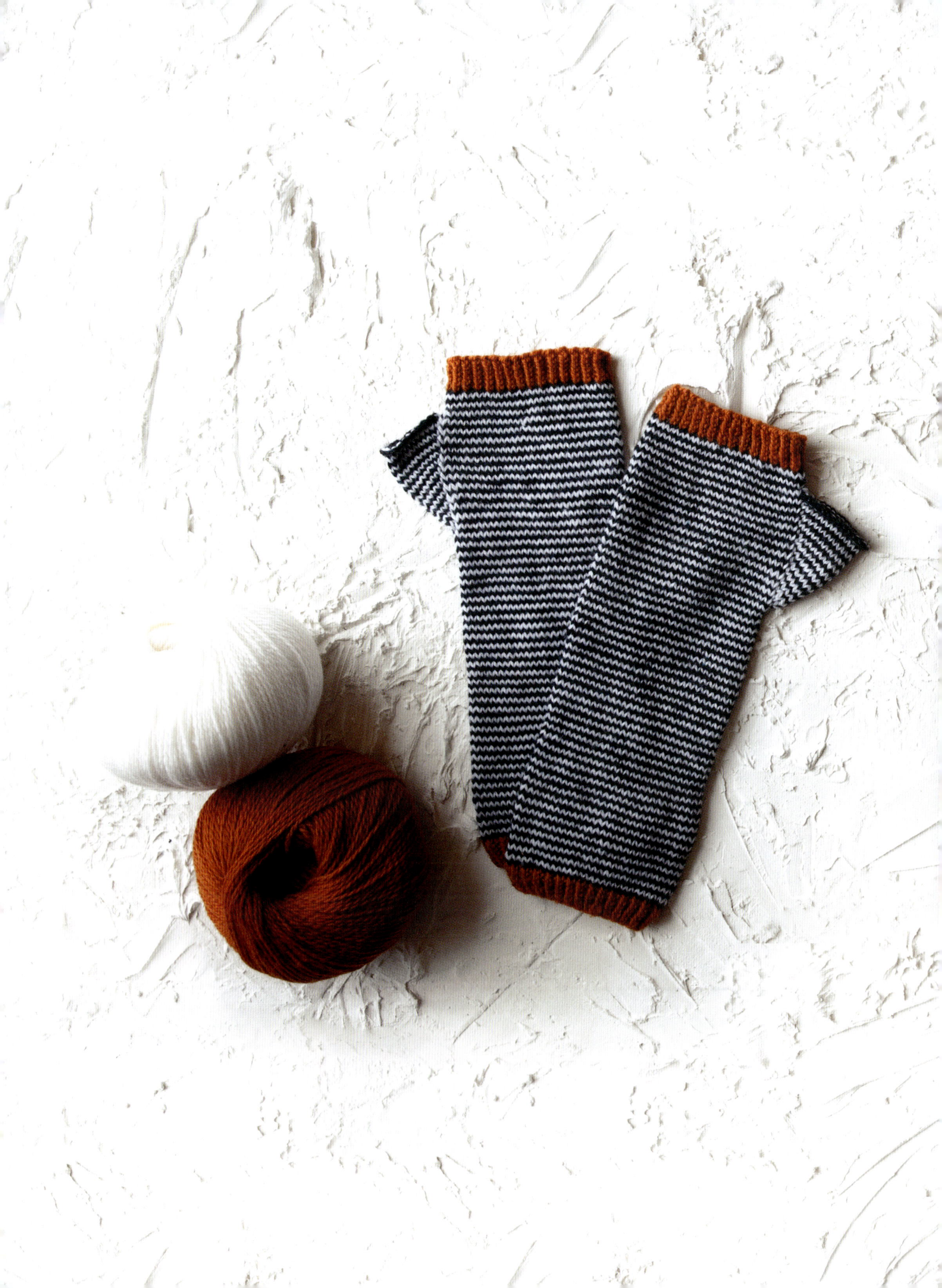

Hands & Feet

CANDY STRIPES FINGERLESS MITTS

by Amanda Carrigan

FINISHED MEASUREMENTS
7" palm circumference, and about 7.5" total length.

YARN
Knit Picks Palette (100% Peruvian Highland Wool; 231 yards/50g):
MC: Almond 24560, and CC: Toffee 25995, 1 ball each

NEEDLES
US 1 (2.25mm) DPNs or circulars for magic loop, or size to obtain gauge

NOTIONS
Yarn Needle
Stitch Markers
Scrap yarn or stitch holder

GAUGE
36 sts and 36 rounds = 4" in stranded St st in the round, unblocked.

For pattern support, contact amlcarrigan@yahoo.com

Candy Stripes Fingerless Mitts

Notes:
Special Stitches
2x2 Ribbing (worked in the round over a multiple of 4 sts):
All Rnds: (K2, P2) to end

The stripes slant in opposite directions on the two mitts, but the construction for each mitt is the same, so both mitts can be worn on either hand. Since the pattern remains the same for each row, just moving one stitch over, you will probably find that these go fairly fast, and don't require paying a lot of attention to the graph.

If you want a larger pair of mitts, go up a needle size. A gauge of about 31 sts / 4" will produce mitts to fit an 8" hand size.

Each pair of mitts requires 140 yards (30g) of MC and 65 yards (14g) of CC. You can get a second pair of mitts out of two balls of Palette if you reverse main and contrast colors for the second pair.

DIRECTIONS
Hand
With MC, CO 64 sts. Divide evenly over 3 or 4 DPNs, PM, and join to work in the round, being careful not to twist.
Rnds 1-15: Work 2x2 ribbing
Rnd 16: K to end

Join CC and begin to work Round 1 from the Left Hand graph.

On round 15 of the graph, place markers before and after the first increased stitch to mark the thumb gusset. Stitches between markers will be your gusset stitches. Make remaining gusset increases inside the markers.

After round 38 of the graph, move the gusset stitches between markers to a waste yarn or stitch holder and continue. *You do not cast on additional stitches over the gap, to maintain the stitch pattern. Just make sure to pull stitches over the gap tight for a few rounds*.

After finishing graph, break CC yarn, and continue with MC only.
Next rnd: K to end
Next 5 rnds: Work 2x2 ribbing

Bind off all stitches in pattern.

Thumb
Transfer the 21 gusset stitches to needles. Pick up 3 additional stitches on hand side. Divide the 24 sts over 3 needles, and join MC to work thumb.
Rnd 1: K to end
Rnds 2-6: Work 2x2 ribbing

Bind off all stitches in pattern.

Finishing
Weave in ends, and block.
Make the second mitt the same as the first, but using Right Hand graph.

Right Hand

46 Candy Stripes Fingerless Mitts

Legend:

- ☐ knit with MC
- ▨ knit with CC
- ▨ No Stitch
  Placeholder - No stitch made.
- M make one
  Make one by lifting strand in between stitch just worked and the next stitch, knit into back of this thread.

Left Hand

Legend:

☐ knit with MC

■ knit with CC

■ No Stitch
Placeholder - No stitch made.

M make one
Make one by lifting strand in between stitch just worked and the next stitch, knit into back of this thread.

Candy Stripes Fingerless Mitts | 47

FRIDA FINGERLESS MITTS

by Laura Graham

FINISHED MEASUREMENTS
8.5" long, from wrist to fingers
Mitts stretch to fit hand circumference 6 – 7"

YARN
Knit Picks Stroll Glimmer (70% Fine Superwash Merino Wool, 25% Nylon, 5% Stellina; 231 yards/50g)
Frost 25495, 1 ball.

NEEDLES
US 2 (3mm) DPNs or one 32" or longer circular needle for Magic Loop technique, or size to obtain gauge

NOTIONS
Yarn Needle
Stitch Markers
Cable needle
Scrap yarn or stitch holder

GAUGE
42 sts and 42 rows = 4" in cable pattern in the round, blocked, unstretched.

For pattern support, contact uclaura98@gmail.com

Frida Fingerless Mitts

Notes:

These mitts are knit in the round, in an alternating cable and rib pattern for the main body of the mitt, and stockinette stitch for the thumb. The thumb is finished with a 2x2 rib. The mitts are worked from the wrists up, and are identical for left and right hands.

Special Stitches

C4R

Place 2 stitches on cable needle and hold in back. Knit next 2 stitches, then knit 2 stitches from cable needle.

Cable Pattern (worked in the round over a multiple of 10 sts)

Rnd 1: (K2, P2, K4, P2) to end.
Rnd 2: Repeat Rnd 1.
Rnd 3: (K2, P2, C4R, P2) to end.
Rnds 4-6: Repeat Rnd 1.

Repeat Rnds 1 – 6 for Cable Pattern.

DIRECTIONS

Mitts (make two)

CO 60 sts. Place marker and join in the round, taking care not to twist stitches.

Rnds 1 – 44: Work 7 full repeats of Cable Pattern, then work Rnds 1 – 2 of Cable Pattern once.

Thumb Gusset

Rnd 45: K1, M1R, work Cable Pattern as established to end - 61 sts.
Rnd 46: K3, work Cable Pattern as established to end.
Rnd 47: K1, M1R, K1, M1L, PM, work Cable Pattern as established to end - 63 sts.
Rnd 48: K to marker, SM, work Cable Pattern as established to end.
Rnd 49: K1, M1R, K to marker, M1L, SM, work Cable Pattern as established to end - 65 sts.
Rnds 50 – 65: Repeat Rnds 48 – 49 eight times more – you should have 81 sts (22 sts before marker) after Rnd 65.
Rnd 66: Repeat Rnd 48.
Rnd 67: K1, place next 21 thumb stitches on a holder or waste yarn, remove marker, K1, P2, K4, P2, (K2, P2, K4, P2) to end – 60 sts on needles.
Rnd 68 – 94: Work Cable Pattern as established.

Bind off.

Thumb

Place held thumb stitches back onto needles. Knit across these 21 sts, pick up and knit 3 sts at thumb opening, join to work in the round – 24 sts.

Rnds 1 - 5: K all sts.
Rnds 7 - 12: (K2, P2) to end.

Bind off.

Finishing

Weave in ends, wash and block mitts, taking care not to stretch widthwise.

HELICAL SOCKS

by Kenny Chua

FINISHED MEASUREMENTS
(Child, Women, Men)

YARN
Knit Picks Stroll Solids (75% Merino, 25% Nylon; 231 yards/50g):
A Forest H 24589, B Rainforest H 25608, C Tranquil 26083 and D Cork 25609, 1 ball each.

NEEDLES
US 2 (2.75 mm) DPNs or two 24" circular needles for two circulars technique, or one 32" or longer circular needle for Magic Loop technique, or size to obtain gauge

NOTIONS
Yarn Needle
Stitch Markers

GAUGE
7.5 sts and 11 rows = 1" over helical St st in the round

For pattern support, contact kenny.chua@hotmail.com

Helical Socks

Notes:
Helical knitting is essentially knitting in the round, until you reach the next color, then just drop the yarn, pick up the new color without twisting and without pulling too tight, and continue knitting until you reach the next color, drop the yarn, pick up the next color, so on and so forth. Do not twist when changing colors.

Use your favorite method of knitting socks. I will try and make the directions as general as possible to accommodate all the techniques.

Assign your colors anyway you like. We're using 4 colors and designate them using A, B, C and D.

All 4 yarns are being worked at once in the helical portion of the knitting. Try and avoid a tangled mess by untwisting the balls of yarn periodically.

Stitch Pattern (1 x 1 Ribbing in the round)
Round 1: *k1, p1; repeat from *
Round 2: repeat round 1

DIRECTIONS
Leg
With Color A, CO 44 (60, 72) sts. Join to work in the round, being careful not to twist, and pm to mark beg of rnd.

Work 1x1 ribbing for 1 (1.25, 1.5)". Attach B and knit 11 (15, 18) sts. Attach C and knit 11 (15, 18) sts. Attach D and knit 11 (15, 18) sts.

After knitting with D, you should have 4 strands of yarn dangling from your knitting. Continue knitting with D until you reach A, drop D and pick up A and knit until you reach B, drop B and knit with C until you reach D, drop D and pick up A until you reach B so on and so forth, in the round, helically.

Knit in this fashion until leg measures 4.5 (6, 6.5)" from CO, ending with B at the beginning of the round. By this time, you should have 3 different colored sections (2 sections would have the same number of stitches and the 3rd section's stitch count is the sum of both of the 2 small sections). There should be 1 color at the beginning of each section but 2 colors at the end of the large section. Using the next color and working only over the big section, work the heel flap as follows:

Heel Flap
Work only with B back and forth for heel flap over 22 (30, 36) sts. Work B as follows:
Row 1 (RS): SL1 as if to purl with yarn in front, *K1, SL 1 as if to knit; repeat from * to last st, K1.
Row 2 (WS): SL1 as if to purl with yarn in front, P20 (28, 34), K1

Repeat rows 1 and 2 10 (14, 17) more times ending with a WS row.

Turning the Heel
Row 1: K13 (17, 20) sts, K2TOG, K1, turn.
Row 2: SL1, P5, SSP, P1, turn.
Row 3: SL1, K6, K2TOG, K1, turn.
Row 4: SL1, P7, SSP, P1, turn.
Row 5: SL1, K8, K2TOG, K1, turn.
Row 6: SL1, P9, SSP, P1, turn.
Row 7: SL1, K10, K2TOG, K1, turn.
(See below for child's final 2 rows)

Row 8: SL1, P11, SSP, P1, turn.
Row 9: SL1, K12, K2TOG, K1, turn.
Row 10: SL1, P13, SSP, P1, turn.
Row 11: SL1, K14, K2TOG, K1, turn.
(See below for women's final 2 rows)

Row 12: SL1, P15, SSP, P1, turn.
Row 13: SL1, K16, K2TOG, K1, turn.
Row 14: SL1, P17, SSP, P1, turn.
(See below for men's final 3 rows)

Final 2 rows of child's heel-turning:
Row 8: SL1, P11, SSP, P1, turn.
Row 9: K14

Final 2 rows of women's heel-turning:
Row 12: SL1, P15, SSP, P1, turn.
Row 13: K18

Final 3 rows of men's heel-turning:
Row 15: SL1, K18, K2TOG, turn.
Row 16: SL1, P18, SSP, turn.
Row 17: SL1, K19

Picking up Gusset sts
With the same needle used for the heel flap, pick up and knit 11 (15, 18) sts in through the loops along the right side of heel flap. In the intersection of the heel flap and the instep, pick up the strand in between and knit into it twisted, place marker. From the other end of the needle, transfer 7 (9, 10) sts to the other needle holding the instep sts. Back to the heel flap needle, attach A and knit across 11 (15, 18) instep sts. You should have now come to the next color and should have 30 (40, 47) sts on the first needle.

Using the other needle, drop A and pick up C and knit across the rest of the instep sts, pm. Drop C and pick up D and, in the intersection of the instep and the bottom of the other side of the heel flap, pick up the strand in between, knit into it twisted. Using D, pick up and knit 11 (15, 18) sts across the other side of the heel flap. Then knit the remaining 7 (9, 10) heel turn sts you transferred from the first needle.

Now you should have 30 (40, 47) sts on each half of the sock, with yarns ready to continue knitting helically.

Gusset
Knit 1 round.
Round 1: K15 (21, 25), K2TOG, K1, sm, knit to 3 sts before next marker, K1, SSK, K15 (21, 25).
Round 2 and all even numbered rounds: Knit
Round 3: K14 (20, 24), K2TOG, K1, sm, knit to 3 sts before next marker, K1, SSK, K14 (20, 24) sts.

Continue knitting helically in this fashion until you have 22 (30, 36) on each half of the sock.

Foot and Toe
Knit helically, for the rest of the foot until you are 2 inches from the toe. Ending with the starting color C on the largest section. With C only, knit all sts and decrease every other round as follows:

Round 1: K8 (12, 15), K2TOG, K2, SSK, K8 (12, 15), K8 (12, 15), K2TOG, K2, SSK, K8 (12, 15).
Round 2 and all even number rounds: Knit.

Repeat rounds 1 and 2 until you have 8 (10, 12) sts left on each half of thesock.

Finishing
Graft toes together using Kitchener st. Weave in all ends.

HELYX FINGERLESS MITTS

by Melanie Berg

FINISHED MEASUREMENTS
Size M: 6" in circumference and 9" in length
Size L: 7.5" in circumference and 9" in length

YARN
Knit Picks Galileo (50% Merino Wool, 50% Viscose from Bamboo; 131 yards/50g):
Firefly 26101, 2 balls

NEEDLES
US 2.5 (3mm) double pointed needles, or size to obtain gauge

NOTIONS
Yarn Needle

GAUGE
16 sts and 20 rows = 2" in St st, blocked
1 row = 2" wide, 20 rows = 2" long, blocked

For pattern support, contact melanie@mairlynd.de

Helyx Fingerless Mitts

Notes:
The Helyx Mitts are worked flat on two needles. Starting with only two stitches, increases are worked until there are ten (eleven) live stitches. Then a spiral is formed and each last RS stitch is attached to the preceding spiral. The mitt then winds itself up the forearm. All stitches are bound off for the thumb opening, cast on again and then the spiral continues its way. Just before reaching the final length, decreases are worked so that the end of the spiral will fit perfectly into shape.

Upper and lower opening are seamed with an I-cord.

Attaching the spiral rows to each other (Join):
Attach the last st of each RS row to the first st of the preceding spiral row as follows:
SL last st of row purlwise wyib, pick up and knit right leg of first st of the preceding spiral row, psso
This technique will be referred to in the directions as "Join".

DIRECTIONS (make 2)
CO 2 sts using the long-tail cast on method.
Setup row (WS): SL 1 purlwise wyif, P1 (2 sts)

Preparing the spiral
Row 1 (RS): SL 1 knitwise wyib, knit to end of row.
Row 2: SL 1 purlwise wyif, purl to end of row.
Rows 3-6: Repeat rows 1-2 two more times.
Row 7: SL 1 knitwise wyib, M1L, knit to end of row. (3 sts)
Row 8: SL 1 purlwise wyif, purl to end of row.
Rows 9-12: Repeat rows 1-2 two more times.
Row 13: SL 1 knitwise wyib, M1L, knit to end of row. (4 sts)
Row 14: SL 1 purlwise wyif, purl to end of row.
Rows 15-18: Repeat rows 1-2 two more times.
Row 19: SL 1 knitwise wyib, YO, knit to end of row. (5 sts)
Row 20: SL 1 purlwise wyif, purl to end of row.
Row 21: K2TOG, YO, knit to end of row.
Row 22: SL 1 purlwise wyif, purl to end of row.
Rows 23-24: Repeat rows 21-22 once more.
Row 25: SL 1 knitwise wyib, K1, YO, knit to end of row. (6 sts)
Row 26: SL 1 purlwise wyif, purl to end of row.
Row 27: SL 1 knitwise wyib, K2TOG, YO, knit to end of row.
Row 28: SL 1 purlwise wyif, purl to end of row.
Rows 29-30: Repeat rows 27-28 once more.
Row 31: SL 1 knitwise wyib, M1L, K2TOG, YO, knit to end of row. (7 sts)
Row 32: SL 1 purlwise wyif, purl to end of row.
Row 33: SL 1 knitwise wyib, K1, K2TOG, YO, knit to end of row.
Row 34: SL 1 purlwise wyif, purl to end of row.
Rows 35-36: Repeat rows 33-34 once more.
Row 37: SL 1 knitwise wyib, M1L, K1, K2TOG, YO, knit to end of row. (8 sts)
Row 38: SL 1 purlwise wyif, purl to end of row.
Row 39: SL 1 knitwise wyib, K2, K2TOG, YO, knit to end of row.
Row 40: SL 1 purlwise wyif, purl to end of row.
Rows 41-42: Repeat rows 39-40 once more.
Row 43: SL 1 knitwise wyib, M1L, K2, K2TOG, YO, knit to end of row. (9 sts)
Row 44: SL 1 purlwise wyif, purl to end of row.
Row 45: SL 1 knitwise wyib, K3, K2TOG, YO, knit to end of row.
Row 46: SL 1 purlwise wyif, purl to end of row.
Rows 47-48: Repeat rows 45-46 once more.
Row 49: SL 1 knitwise wyib, M1L, K3, K2TOG, YO, knit to end of row. (10 sts)
Row 50: SL 1 purlwise wyif, purl to end of row.
Row 51: SL 1 knitwise wyib, K4, K2TOG, YO, knit to end of row.
Row 52: SL 1 purlwise wyif, purl to end of row.
Rows 53-54: Repeat rows 51-52 once more.

Size L only:
Row 55: SL 1 knitwise wyib, M1L, K4, K2TOG, YO, knit to end of row. (11 sts)
Row 56: SL 1 purlwise wyif, purl to end of row.
Row 57: SL 1 knitwise wyib, K5, K2TOG, YO, knit to end of row.
Row 58: SL 1 purlwise wyif, purl
Rows 59-60: Repeat rows 57-58 once more.

Working the spiral
Form a tube with your knitting. From now on, the last stitch of every RS row will be attached to the preceding spiral.

Row 1 (RS): SL 1 knitwise wyib, K4 (5), K2TOG, YO, K2, Join.
Row 2: SL 1 purlwise wyif, purl to end of row.

Repeat rows 1-2 until mitt measures 6" from CO edge.

Thumb gusset
BO all sts as follows:

K1, [K1, SSK] repeat until all sts are bound off. Break yarn and pull through last st.

CO 10 (11) sts using the long-tail cast on method. Join last st with the preceding spiral as described in Notes, attaching the spiral rows to each other. 10 (11) sts.

Setup row (WS): SL 1 purlwise wyif, purl to end of row.
Row 1 (RS): SL 1 knitwise wyib, K4 (5), K2TOG, YO, K2, Join.
Row 2: SL 1 purlwise wyif, purl to end of row.

Repeat rows 1-2 35 more times.

End of the spiral
For size L only:
Row 1 (RS): SL 1 knitwise wyib, K2TOG, K3, K2TOG, YO, K2, Join. (10 sts)
Row 2: SL 1 purlwise wyif, purl to end of row.
Row 3: SL 1 knitwise wyib, K4, K2TOG, YO, K2, Join.
Row 4: SL 1 purlwise wyif, purl to end of row.
Rows 5-6: Repeat rows 3-4 once more.

For size M, beg with row 7:
Row 7 (RS): SL 1 knitwise wyib, K2TOG, K2, K2TOG, YO, K2, Join. (9 sts)
Row 8: SL 1 purlwise wyif, purl to end of row.
Row 9: SL 1 knitwise wyib, K3, K2TOG, YO, K2, Join.
Row 10: SL 1 purlwise wyif, purl to end of row.
Rows 11-12: Repeat rows 9-10 once more.
Row 13: SL 1 knitwise wyib, K2TOG, K1, K2TOG, YO, K2, Join. (8 sts)

Row 14: SL 1 purlwise wyif, purl to end of row.
Row 15: SL 1 knitwise wyib, K2, K2TOG, YO, K2, Join.
Row 16: SL 1 purlwise wyif, purl to end of row.
Rows 17-18: Repeat rows 15-16 once more.
Row 19: SL 1 knitwise wyib, K2TOG, K2TOG, YO, K2, Join. (7 sts)
Row 20: SL 1 purlwise wyif, purl to end of row.
Row 21: SL 1 knitwise wyib, K1, K2TOG, YO, K2, Join.
Row 22: SL 1 purlwise wyif, purl to end of row.
Rows 23-24: Repeat rows 21-22 once more.
Row 25: SL 1 knitwise wyib, K3TOG, YO, K2, Join. (6 sts)
Row 26: SL 1 purlwise wyif, purl to end of row.
Row 27: SL 1 knitwise wyib, K2TOG, YO, K2, Join.
Row 28: SL 1 purlwise wyif, purl to end of row.
Rows 29-30: Repeat rows 27-28 once more.
Row 31: K3TOG, YO, K2, Join. (5 sts)
Row 32: SL 1 purlwise wyif, purl to end of row.
Row 33: K2TOG, YO, K2, Join.
Row 34: SL 1 purlwise wyif, purl to end of row.
Rows 35-36: Repeat rows 33-34 once more.
Row 37: SL 1 knitwise wyib, K2TOG, K1, Join. (4 sts)
Row 38: SL 1 purlwise wyif, purl to end of row.
Row 39: SL 1 knitwise wyib, K2, Join.

Row 40: SL 1 purlwise wyif, purl to end of row.
Rows 41-42: Repeat rows 39-40 once more.
Row 43: SL 1 knitwise wyib, K2TOG, Join. (3 sts)
Row 44: SL 1 purlwise wyif, purl to end of row.
Row 45: SL 1 knitwise wyib, K1, Join.
Row 46: SL 1 purlwise wyif, purl to end of row.
Rows 47-48: Repeat rows 45-46 once more.

I-cord seam

Work the following steps very loosely. If necessary change to larger needles:

[with left tip of LH needle, pick up right leg of first st of the preceding spiral row, move sts to right tip of LH needle, K2, K2TOG]. (3 sts) Repeat until whole upper opening of the mitt is seamed with an I-cord.

Knit the last 3 sts together, break yarn and pull through last st.

CO 3 sts using the long-tail cast on method and seam lower opening the same way.

Finishing

Weave in all ends. Gently wash and block.

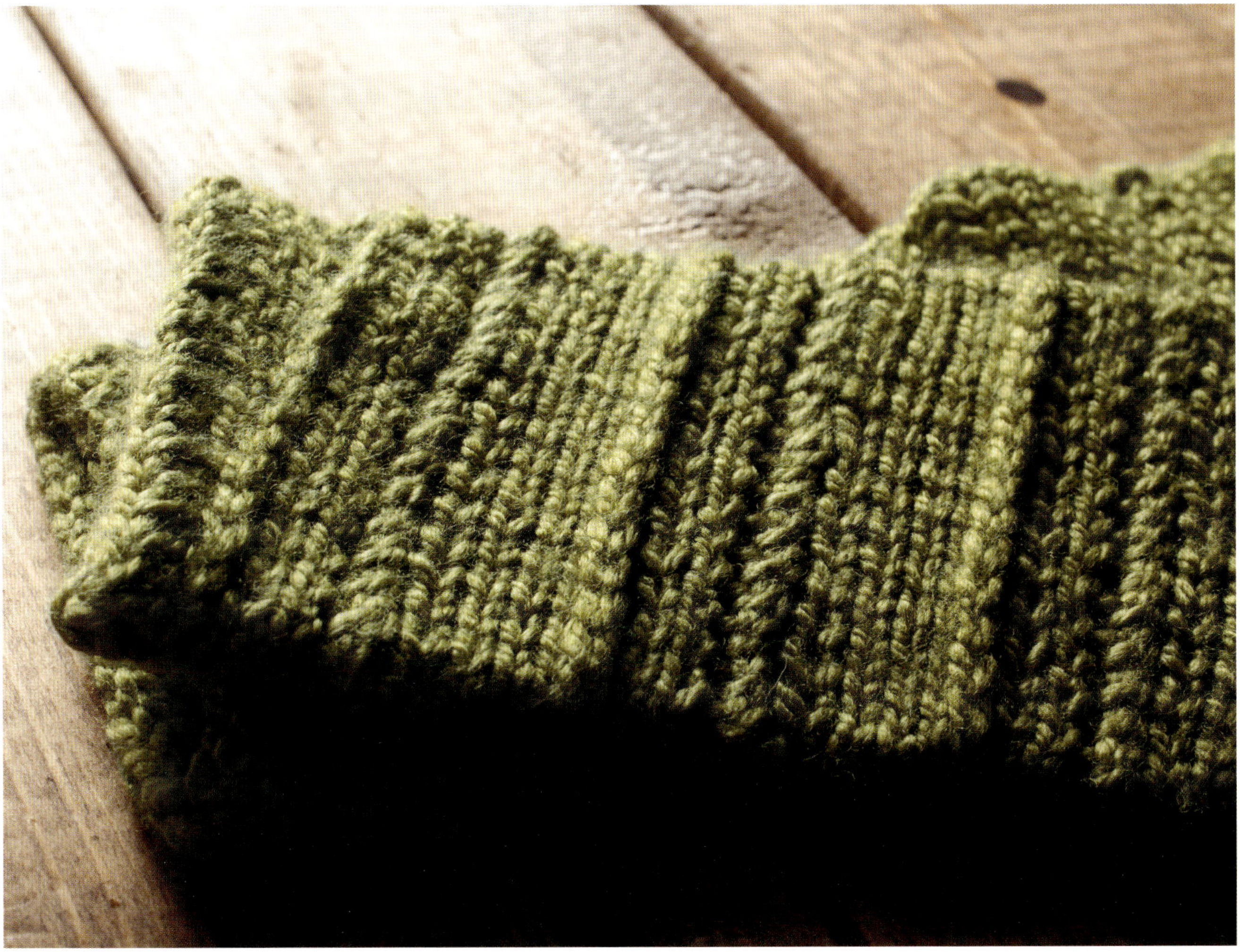

SCRUNCHY OMBRE ARM WARMERS

by Amanda Schwabe

FINISHED MEASUREMENTS
6.5 (7.5, 8.5)" finished hand circumference; garment is meant to be worn with up to 0.5" of negative ease around the hand.
3.25 (3.75, 4.25)" wide across hand; 10" long.

YARN
Knit Picks Palette (100% Peruvian Highland Wool; 231 yards/50g):
Ombre Stripes version: A Celadon Heather 24254, B Midnight Heather 25540, C Douglas Fir 26046, D Sagebrush 25549, E Opal Heather 25096, F Clarity 25548, 10g ea.
Simple Stripe version:
Knit Picks Palette (100% Peruvian Highland Wool; 231 yards/50g): MC Midnight Heather 25540, 15-20g; CC1 Clarity 25548, 15-20g, CC2 Masala 24248, 10g.

NEEDLES
US 2 (2.75mm) DPNs or two 24" circular needles for two circulars technique, or one 32" or longer circular needle for Magic Loop technique, or size to obtain gauge

NOTIONS
Yarn Needle
Stitch Markers
Scrap yarn or stitch holder

GAUGE
32 sts and 44 rows = 4" in St st in the round, alternating colors each round.

For pattern support, contact amandaschwabe@sympatico.ca

Scrunchy Ombre Arm Warmers

Notes:
These arm warmers are knit from the cuff up in mostly St st, with an offset thumb gusset. The cuff is extra long so the fabric can be worn scrunched.

The Twisted-Rib edges at bottom and top are worked in one color only; the St st body is worked by alternating between two colors every round, carrying the yarn up between stripes instead of cutting it. This forms overlapping stripes of color that blend into each other, and results in fewer ends to sew in. Beautiful stripes can be made with only the tiniest bits of leftover yarns from your stash. Use these color instructions, or make up your own palette. By arranging your stash from light to dark, or with arcs on the color wheel, you can create truly beautiful and surprising blends of color.

Directions are written for the basic structure, and specific instructions for the color stripes are in the Notes below.

Special Stitches:
Twisted-Rib Pattern (in the round over an even number of sts)
All Rnds: (K1tbl, P1) to end.

Stockinette Stitch (St st)
All Rnds: K to end.

Ombre Stripe Color Instructions
Using A, cast on and work Twisted-Rib according to Directions.

Stripe Section 1: Cut yarn and join Color B. Work Round 7 in B, then, without cutting B, join C and work next round with C. Alternate using B and C every round until their stripe measures 2.25", ending after C.

Stripe Section 2: Cut B and join D. Continue, alternating C and D every round until their stripe measures 2.25", ending after D.

Stripe Section 3: Cut C and join E. Continue, alternating D and E every round until their stripe measures 2.25", ending after E. (Note: The Thumb Gusset will begin during this stripe and continue into the next stripe.)

Stripe Section 4: Cut D and join F. Continue, alternating E and F every round until their stripe measures about 2.5", ending after F.

Cuff: At this point, you should be ready to begin the Twisted-Rib cuff around the hand. Cut E and F. Join A to work the Twisted-Rib section.

Simple Stripe Color Instructions
Using CC2, cast on and work Twisted-Rib according to Directions. Cut CC2.

Join MC and work Round 7. Without cutting MC, join CC1 and work one round of St st. Continue alternating MC and CC1 every round in St st, including Thumb instructions, until you reach the Twisted-Rib section on the hand.

Cut both colors and join CC2, then work in Twisted-Rib to end.

DIRECTIONS
CO 50 (58, 66) sts. PM and join for working in the round, being careful not to twist the sts.

Rnds 1-6: Work in Twisted-Rib Pattern.
Rnd 7: (K1tbl, K1) to end. (See Color Instructions. This round is not worked in the cuff color.)

Work in St st (see Color Instructions) until piece measures 7" from cast on edge.

Thumb Gusset
Left Hand
Set-Up Rnd: K 19 (23, 27) sts, PM, M1, PM, K to end.

Right Hand
Set-Up Rnd: K 31 (35, 39) sts, PM, M1, PM, K to end.

Both Hands
Rnd A: K to end, slipping markers.
Rnd B: K to marker, SM, M1L, K to marker, M1R, SM, K to end.

Repeat Rnds A and B until there are 23 (27, 31) sts between markers after completing a Rnd B.

Divide Thumb
K to marker, place sts between markers onto waste yarn, K to end, removing thumb markers as you go.

Hand
Work in St st for 6 more rounds, maintaining the stripe pattern as established. Cut yarn. Join Cuff color (See Color Instructions).

Work in Twisted-Rib Pattern for 6 rounds. Bind off in pattern.

Thumb
Put the thumb sts from the waste yarn back onto your needles for working in the round. Attach yarn (use the next color in the sequence you've chosen) and use it to bind off all sts knitwise.

Finishing
Weave in ends, using them to close any gaps between the thumb and hand.

SELBU TULIP MITTENS

by Geoff Hunnicutt

FINISHED SIZE
Women's medium to large glove
Length: 11.5 inches long, from cuff to fingertip.
Width: 3.5 inches wide across the palm.

YARN
Knit Picks Palette (100% Peruvian Highland Wool; 231 yards/50g):
MC: Garnet Heather 24015, 1 skein
CC: Suede 24242, 1 skein

NEEDLES
US 2 (3mm) DPNs or two 24" circular needles for two circulars technique, or one 32" or longer circular needle for Magic Loop technique, or size to obtain gauge.
US 1 (2.5mm) DPNs or circular needles for two circulars technique, or one 32" or longer circular needle for Magic Loop technique.

NOTIONS
Yarn Needle
Stitch Markers
Scrap yarn or stitch holder
Spare DPNs
Straight Pins

GAUGE
36 sts and 34 rows = 4" measured over cuff using US 2.

For pattern support, contact buckstrong@wildhorsefiberworks.com

Selbu Tulip Mittens

Notes:

The Selbu Tulip Mittens are a cute retro take on traditional Selbuvotter mittens. The back of the hand has a fun mid-century tulip design, while the palm uses a traditional Selbu pattern. The thumb design mimics that of the mittens and has a gusset. To add to the fun, these mittens have a gauntlet cuff with a picot edge.

Stitch Pattern (worked in the round over an even number of stitches.)

This is color work knitting which requires the knitter to carry two different strands of yarn while knitting. Also, the knitter should know how to carry floats on the back of their knitting. For a good tutorial, please go to http://www.youtube.com/watch?v=rcrRujO2Olo

When folding the work to form the picot hem, knitters may find it useful to pin the hem in place before knitting the edge to the body of the work.

DIRECTIONS
Cuff

With smaller needles and MC, cast on 72 stitches, place marker and join circularly, being careful not to twist the stitches. If using DPNs, divide stitches evenly onto 4 needles and join circularly. Knit 6 rounds. Next round, *k2tog, yo; repeat to end. This will be the picot hem edge. Knit 6 rounds. Next round, fold along the hem so that the purl sides are facing each other and the cast on row is behind the live stitches on your needles. Using the right hand needle and starting with the first cast on stitch, pick up a stitch from the cast on row and place it on the left hand needle, k2tog. Continue in this manner until the end of the round. This will join the edge to the work. Change to larger needles and knit 6 more rounds then work Chart A, repeating the chart across all the stitches. With MC, knit 2 rounds. Next round decrease as follows k4, k2tog, 12 times (60 stitches). Knit 3 rounds. Remove marker, knit 3 and replace marker. This is the new beginning of the round and lines up charts.

Lower Hand and Thumb Gusset

Begin Chart B. Please note that Chart B has charts for both the right and left hand. Work one palm (stitches 1-35 or 75-109) and the back pattern (stitches 36-74) for each mitten.

Setting the Thumb Aside

Continue knitting Chart B until you reach Row 9. There are 15 stitches that are lined through. Slip these 15 stitches onto a scrap piece of yarn and cast on 15 stitches onto the right hand needle using the backward loop method. Be sure to cast on in pattern as indicated on the chart. This will give a smooth pattern transition from the palm to the thumb. Work the rest of the chart as indicated. To close up the top of the mitten, break off the yarn leaving about a 6 inch tail. Thread the yarn onto a tapestry needle and then thread the yarn through the remaining stitches; pull the yarn tight. Thread the yarn through the top of the mitten to the wrong side. Turn the mitten inside out and weave in ends.

Thumb

Turn the mitten palm up, slip the stitches from the waste yarn onto needles. Pick up 2 stitches from the side of the thumb hole. Now, pick up 15 stitches from the stitches you cast on earlier and 2 two stitches from the side of the thumb hole. Work Chart C. To close up the top of the thumb, break off the yarn leaving about a 6 inch tail. Thread the yarn onto a tapestry needle and then thread the yarn through the remaining stitches; pull the yarn tight. Thread the yarn through the top of the thumb to the wrong side. Turn the mitten inside out and weave in ends and close up any holes around the thumb.

Finishing

Wet blocking is extremely important with color work knitting. It evens out the little puckers that happen as you knit. Give the finished mittens a good long soak in hot soapy water; then another long soak in hot water to rinse. Roll the mittens up in a clean towel and press as much water out as possible. You may want to do this a couple of times with a new dry towel each time.

Your mittens should be damp. Now pin your mittens to the desired measurements. Be sure to stretch the mittens so that there are no puckers and the material looks smooth. If you are the intended wearer, you may want to put the damp mittens on and give them a good stretch over your hand before pinning them down.

Chart B

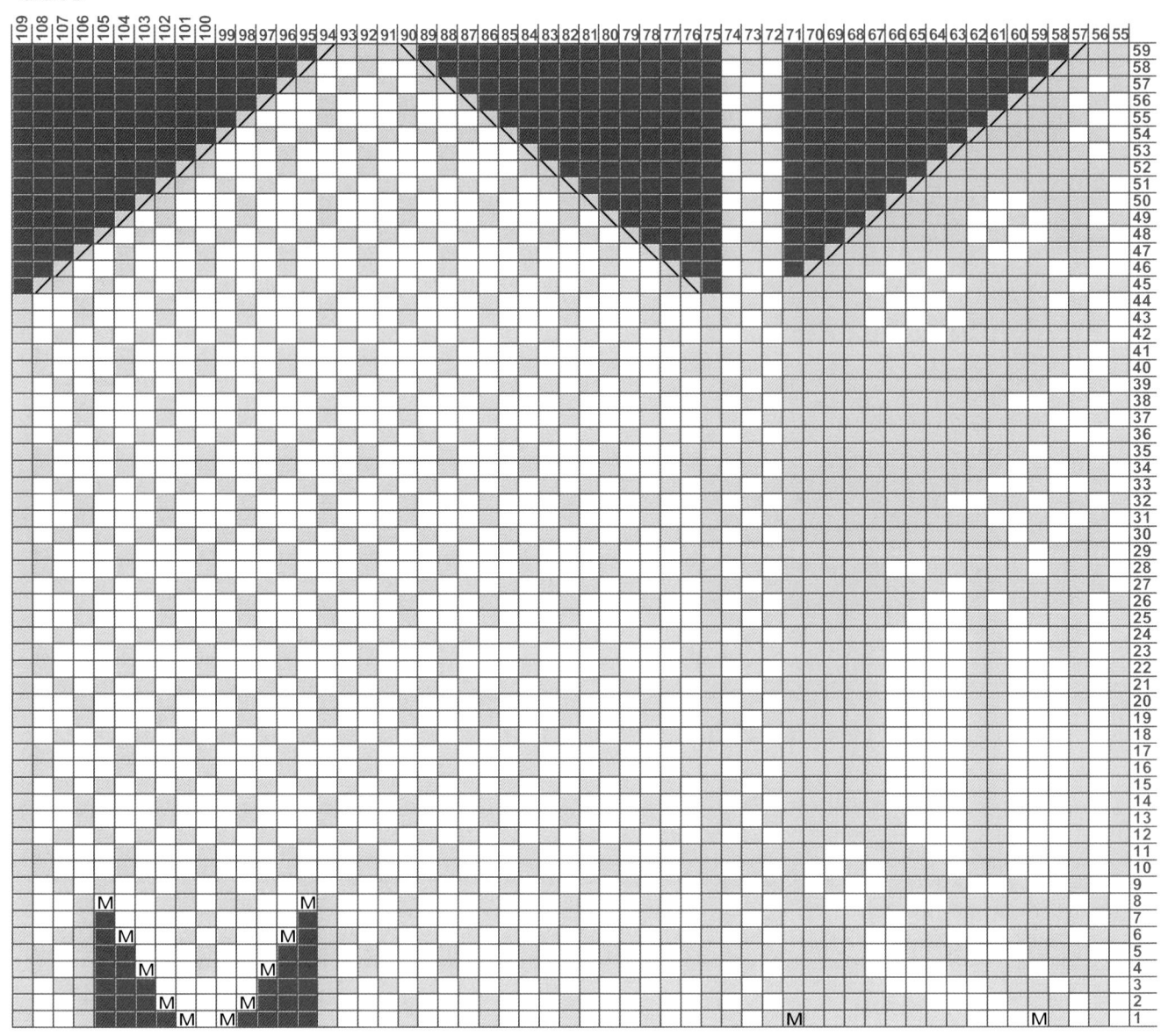

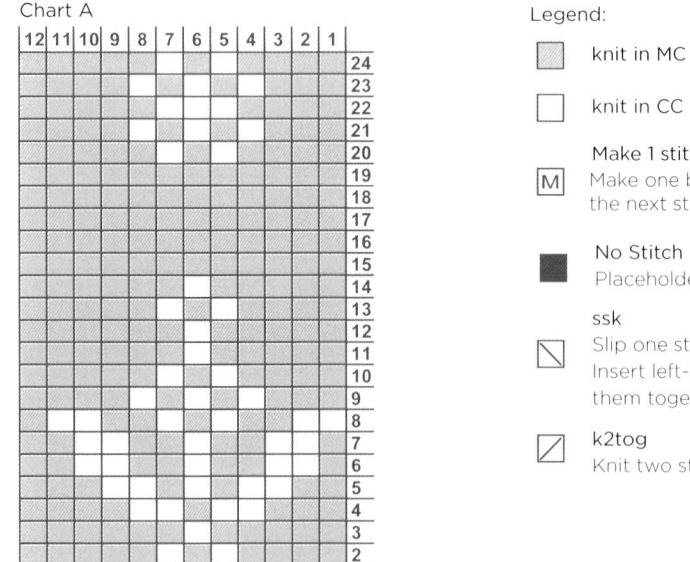

Chart A

Legend:

- ▢ knit in MC
- ▢ knit in CC
- **Make 1 stitch**
  M — Make one by lifting strand in between stitch just worked and the next stitch, knit into back of this thread.
- **No Stitch**
  Placeholder - No stitch made.
- **ssk**
  Slip one stitch as if to knit, Slip another stitch as if to knit. Insert left-hand needle into front of these 2 stitches and knit them together
- **k2tog**
  Knit two stitches together as one stitch

60 | Selbu Tulip Mittens

Chart C

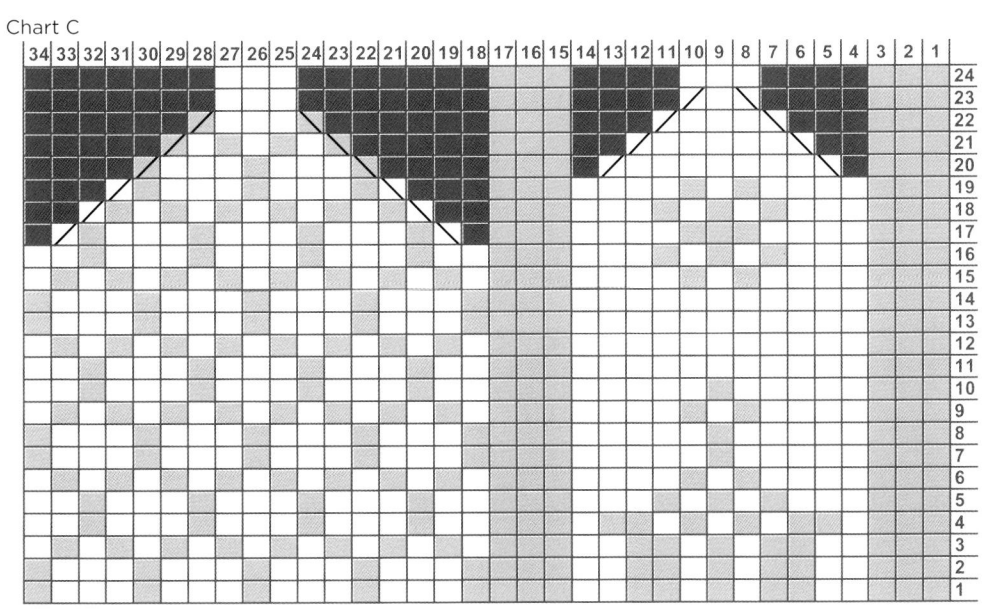

Selbu Tulip Mittens | 61

Hats

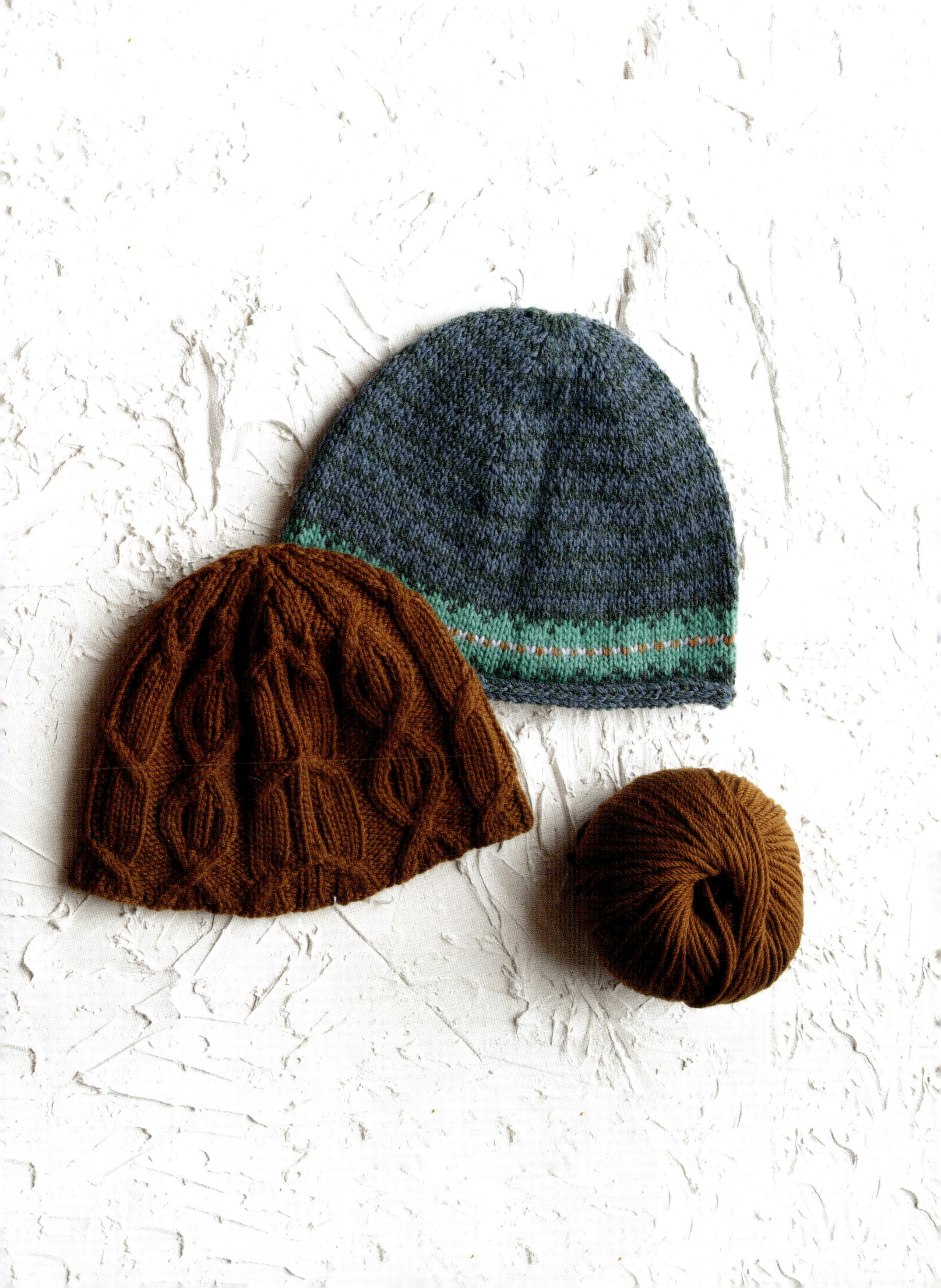

AGAMENTICUS HAT

by Angela Baldi

FINISHED MEASUREMENTS
Finished hat circumference: 16.75 (18.25, 20, 22.25)"; worn with 1-2" negative ease.

YARN
For 16.75" and 18.25" hats:
Knit Picks Wool of the Andes Sport (100% Peruvian Highland Wool, 137 yards/50 g), CC1: Papaya Heather 25301, CC2: Mai Tai Heather 25307, CC3: Oyster Heather 25276, 1 skein each
For 20" and 22.5" hats:
Knit Picks Wool of the Andes (100% Peruvian Highland Wool, 110 yards/50 g), CC1: Midnight Heather 25640, CC3: Fjord Heather 25647, CC2: Clarity 25632, 1 skein each

NEEDLES
US 5 (3.75mm) [6 (4mm), 8 (5mm), 9 (5.5mm)] 16" circular needles, or size to obtain gauge
US 5 (3.75mm) [6 (4mm), 8 (5mm), 9 (5.5mm)] DPNs, or two 24" circular needles for two circulars technique, or one 32" or longer circular needle for Magic Loop technique, or size to obtain gauge

NOTIONS
Yarn Needle
1 Stitch Marker
4 safety pins or locking stitch markers

GAUGE
In stranded St st in the round:
16.75": 24 sts / 24 rows = 4" in sport
18.25": 22 sts / 22 rows = 4" in sport
20": 20 sts / 20.5 rows = 4" in worsted
22.25": 18 sts / 20 rows = 4" in worsted

For pattern support, contact pumpkinpiebaby@gmail.com

Agamenticus Hat

Notes:

This hat is worked in the round from the brim up. Although the hat uses three colors, only two are stranded at a time. The four different sizes are achieved by using either a sport weight wool at two different gauges for the two smaller sizes, or a worsted weight wool at two different gauges for the two larger sizes. The gender neutral design, range of sizes, and options you have when choosing colors make this hat perfect for anyone in your family. The ear flaps are picked up and knit in seed stitch after the body of the hat is done. Finish the ear flaps with either an i-cord or pompoms.

Special Stitches
Seed Stitch (worked in the round over an odd number of sts)
Rnd 1: *K1, p1; repeat from * to last st, k1.
Rnd 2: *P1, k1; repeat from * to last st, p1.
Repeat Rnds 1 - 2 for pattern.

A note about stranding yarn
There are several rows in the chart where you will strand one of the yarns across 7 or 9 sts and it's best to catch those up into the inside of the fabric somehow. I experimented with a few different methods and found this one to work best: Work a row of the Agamenticus Chart. On the next row, at the halfway point of a long strand, reach down inside the hat and pick up the strand onto your left needle. The right side of the strand should sit on the front side of your needle. Knit the strand and the next stitch on your needle together, like k2tog, but you won't be decreasing a stitch. Repeat for any long strands.

DIRECTIONS

Using your 16" circular needle, CO 101 sts with CC1 using the long tail cast on method. PM to denote beginning of rnd and join in the rnd, being careful not to twist your sts.

Rnd 1: Work Rnd 1 of seed stitch, placing removable markers after 11, 30, 70, and 89 sts to mark the position of the ear flaps.
Rnd 2: Work Rnd 2 of seed stitch.
Rnd 3: Work Rnd 1 of seed stitch.
Rnd 4: Work Rnd 2 of seed stitch to last 2 sts, p2tog - 100 sts.

Work Rnds 1 - 24 of the Agamenticus Chart.

Break CC1 and CC3, and continue with CC2 only.

Next Rnd: K all sts.

Decreases
The top of the hat has 10 wedges - 1 st will be decreased in each wedge, for a total of 10 sts decreased in each rnd. Switch to DPN's or 2 circs or magic loop when you need to.

For the 16.75" hat only, omit Rnds 8 and 10.

Rnd 1: *K2tog, k8; repeat from * to end of rnd - 90 sts.
Rnd 2: K all sts.
Rnd 3: *K2tog, k7; repeat from * to end of rnd - 80 sts.
Rnd 4: K all sts.
Rnd 5: *K2tog, k6; repeat from * to end of rnd - 70 sts.
Rnd 6: K all sts.
Rnd 7: *K2tog, k5; repeat from * to end of rnd - 60 sts.
Rnd 8: K all sts.
Rnd 9: *K2tog, k4; repeat from * to end of rnd - 50 sts.
Rnd 10: K all sts.
Rnd 11: *K2tog, k3; repeat from * to end of rnd - 40 sts.
Rnd 12: *K2tog, k2; repeat from * to end of rnd - 30 sts.
Rnd 13: *K2tog, k1; repeat from * to end of rnd - 20 sts.
Rnd 14: *K2tog; repeat from * to end of rnd - 10 sts.
Rnd 15: *K2tog; repeat from * to end of rnd - 5 sts.

Break yarn and draw through 5 sts, closing the top of the hat. Weave in ends.

Earflaps

With CC1 and RS facing, pick up 19 sts between the first 2 markers you placed on your cast on row.
Row 1 (WS): *K1, p1; rep from * to last st, k1.
Rows 2 - 3: Rep Row 1.
Row 4 (RS): P1, k2tog, *p1, k1; rep from * to last 4 sts, p1, k2tog, p1 - 17 sts.
Row 5 - 7: *P1, k1; rep from * to last st, p1.
Row 8: K1, p2tog, *k1, p1; rep from * to last 4 sts, k1, p2tog, k1 - 15 sts.
Row 9 - 11: *K1, p1; rep from * to last st, k1.
Row 12: P1, k2tog, *p1, k1; rep from * to last 4 sts, p1, k2tog, p1 - 13 sts.
Row 13: *P1, k1; rep from * to last st, p1.
Row 14: K1, p2tog, *k1, p1; rep from * to last 4 sts, k1, p2tog, k1 - 11 sts.
Row 15: *K1, p1; rep from * to last st, k1.
Row 16: P1, k2tog, *p1, k1; rep from * to last 4 sts, p1, k2tog, p1 - 9 sts.
Row 17: *P1, k1; rep from * to last st, p1.
Row 18: K1, p2tog, k1, p1, k1, p2tog, k1 - 7 sts.
Row 19: *K1, p1; rep from * to last st, k1.
Row 20: P1, k2tog, p1, k2tog, p1 - 5 sts.
Row 21: P1, k1, p1, k1, p1.
Row 22: K2tog, p1, k2tog - 3 sts.

If you are going to finish your earflaps with an i-cord, work a 3 st i-cord for as long as desired.

Otherwise, BO all sts in pattern.
Make a 2" pompom using all three colors of yarn from the hat. Sew the pompom onto the bottom of the ear flap.

Repeat for the 2nd earflap, picking up 19 sts between the 3rd and 4th markers you placed on your cast on row.

Finishing

Weave in your ends, wash, and block gently.

Agamenticus Chart

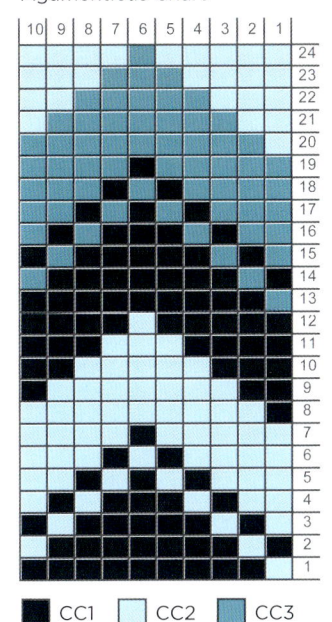

■ CC1 ☐ CC2 ▦ CC3

CHERRY BLOSSOM HEADBAND

by Robin Allen

FINISHED MEASUREMENTS
19" (48 cm) circumference, unstretched.

YARN
Knit Picks Wool of the Andes Sport (100% Peruvian wool; 137yd/50g): Sagebrush 25658, 1 ball.

NEEDLES
US 4 (3.5mm) 16" circular needle, or two 24" circular needles for two circulars technique, or one 32" or longer circular for Magic Loop, or size to obtain gauge.

NOTIONS
Stitch Marker
Yarn Needle

GAUGE
24 sts/33 rows = 4" in Stitch pattern, blocked.

For pattern support, contact atexasgirl_26@yahoo.com

Cherry Blossom Headband

Notes:

This lace headband includes both written and charted instructions and can be knit in a couple of hours.

Seed Stitch

Round 1: *K1, P1. Repeat from * to end of round.
Round 2: *P1, K1. Repeat from * to end of round.

Stitch Pattern (Multiple of 11)
Round 1: *K10, P1; rep from *.
Round 2 (and all even rounds): *K10, P1; rep from *.
Round 3: *K1, (YO, K1) 3 times, (SSK) 3 times, P1; rep from *.
Round 5: *K1, (K1, YO) 3 times, (SSK) 3 times, P1; rep from *.
Round 7: *K1, (YO, K1) 3 times, (SSK) 3 times, P1; rep from *.
Round 9: *K1, (K1, YO) 3 times, (SSK) 3 times, P1; rep from *.
Round 11: *K1, (YO, K1) 3 times, (SSK) 3 times, P1; rep from *.
Round 13: *K10, P1; rep from *.
Round 15: *(K2tog) 3 times, (K1, YO) 3 times, K1, P1; rep from *.
Round 17: *(K2tog) 3 times, (YO, K1) 3 times, K1, P1; rep from *.
Round 19: *(K2tog) 3 times, (K1, YO) 3 times, K1, P1; rep from *.
Round 21: *(K2tog) 3 times, (YO, K1) 3 times, K1, P1; rep from *.
Round 23: *(K2tog) 3 times, (K1, YO) 3 times, K1, P1; rep from *.
Round 25: *K10, P1; rep from *.

DIRECTIONS

Using a stretchy cast-on (I used the German long-tail cast-on), CO 99 sts. PM and join for working in the round, being careful not to twist the line of sts.

Work 2 rounds in Seed stitch.
Work rounds 1–25 of Stitch pat using chart or written instructions.
Work 2 rounds in Seed stitch.

Finishing

Loosely BO all sts. Weave in ends and block to measurements.

Cherry Blossom

Legend:

☐ knit

● purl

◯ yo
Yarn Over

╲ ssk
Slip one stitch as if to knit, Slip another stitch as if to knit. Insert left-hand needle into front of these 2 stitches and knit them together

╱ k2tog
Knit two stitches together as one stitch

COLOR HARMONY CAP

by Lisa McFetridge

FINISHED MEASUREMENTS
Child (Adult, Adult Large): 7.5 (8.5, 8.5)" in height, 17 (19, 21)" in circumference

YARN
Knit Picks Wool of the Andes Worsted (100% Peruvian Highland Wool; 110 yards/50g):
MC: Noble Heather 25990, 50 (55, 60) yards
CC1: Cadet 25070, 40 (45, 50) yards
CC2: Tranquil 25981, 20 (22, 25) yards
CC3: Persimmon 24280 ~3 yards
CC4: Clarity 25632 ~3 yards
Largest size uses a total of 65 grams of yarn.

NEEDLES
US 7 (4.5mm) 24" circular needles, or size needed to obtain gauge
Same size DPNs as above for decreasing
Seam Needle
Stitch Markers
Size G Crochet hook (used for optional Fairy Pull only)

GAUGE
21 sts and 24 rows = 4" in stranded St st in the round, blocked

For pattern support, contact Lisagmc@aol.com

Color Harmony Cap

Notes:

I call this cap "Color Harmony" because it is my way of showing that any color can be made to work with any other colors in knitting, as long as there is balance. Things don't have to "match" - they just have to "go" with each other. If the two main colors are used at the brim of the cap and over the border, the border can be almost any other combination of colors, and it will work! Some of my favorite hats are designed with this "mantra" in mind.

Stranded knitting is often something accomplished knitters are a bit afraid of due to floats, carries and charts. Color Harmony Cap is a great "first" stranded project as there are no carries, no charts needed and it is worked in the round, so the knitter is always looking at and working on the front of the cap. The longest "float" is over 3 stitches, it occurs in the almond border, just remember don't pull the unused color tightly - in stranding LOOSE is always better than tight. The fabric needs to retain its stretch. All other color changes are one stitch, so this cap is a breeze. The cap begins with a braided brim. The braid lends stability to the brim, keeps it flat and firm. Don't let the braid "spook" you. It is one round of knit and two rounds of purl, that's it.

On each round, the color used is listed within '[]' before the color switch.

On solid color rounds, there is no need to carry the unused color, just pick it up on the necessary round from below.

Use M1 for increases unless otherwise noted.

Special Stitches:
Ziggy Stripes:
Rnd 1: *[MC] K1, [CC1] K1, rep from * around.
Rnd 2: [CC1] K around.
Rnd 3: *[CC1] K1, [MC] K1, rep from * around.
Rnd 4: [MC] K around.

Rep Rnds 1 – 4 for pattern.

DIRECTIONS
Hat Body
Note: The following two links show the two-color long-tail cast-on and the braid.

http://www.youtube.com/watch?v=hdECziCsQOE Two Color Long Tail Cast On

http://www.youtube.com/watch?v=QiH6HCjr3zo Knitting a Braided Edge

If you are knitting the braid correctly, the yarns will become very twisted in the second and third rounds. Stop and "untwist" them by letting the needles dangle while holding one strand of yarn in each hand and pulling them gently apart. Be sure to move last color used strand in the proper direction before continuing on.

Braid
Cast on 84 (96, 108) sts using MC & CC1 and two-color long-tail cast-on. Place marker and join on Rnd 1.
Rnd 1: *[MC] K1, [CC1] K1, rep from * around.
Rnd 2: *[MC] P1, move yarn just used to LEFT, [CC1] P1, move yarn just used to the LEFT, rep from * around.
Rnd 3: *[MC] P1, move yarn just used to the RIGHT, [CC1] P1, move yarn just used to the RIGHT, rep from * around.
Rnd 4: [MC] K around.
Rnd 5: [MC] *K 21(24, 27), M1, rep from * around - (88, 100, 112) sts.
Rnd 6: * [CC2] K1, [MC] K1, rep from * around.
Rnd 7: *[MC] K1, [CC2] K3, rep from * around.
Rnds 8 – 9: [CC2] K around.
Rnd 10: *[CC3] K1, [CC4] K1, rep from * around.
Rnds 11 – 12: [CC2] K around.
Rnd 13: *[MC] K1, [CC2] K3, rep from * around.
Rnd 14: * [CC2] K1, [MC] K1, rep from * around.
Rnd 15: [MC] K around, INCREASING 2 sts evenly for Child size and DECREASING 2 sts evenly for Adult Large size. K around for Adult size. Work increases as M1 and decreases as K2tog. - 90, (100, 110) sts.

Work in Ziggy Stripes pattern until hat body measures 4.5 (5, 5)" or until 3 (3.25, 3.5)" less than desired final length, ending with a Rnd 3.

Top Decrease:
Note: All decrease rnds are worked on solid color rnds.

Change to DPN's when needed to complete decreases.

Rnd 1: [MC] *K2Tog, K 14 (16, 18), SSK, rep from * around - 80 (90, 100) sts.
Rnds 2 – 4: Work Rnds 1 – 3 of Ziggy Stripes pattern as established.
Rnd 5: [MC] *K2Tog, K 12 (14, 16), SSK, rep from * around – 70 (80, 90) sts.
Rnds 6 – 8: Work Rnds 1 – 3 of Ziggy Stripes pattern as established.
Rnd 9: [MC] *K2Tog, K 10 (12, 14), SSK, rep from * around – 60 (70, 80) sts.
Rnds 10 – 12: Work Rnds 1 – 3 of Ziggy Stripes pattern as established.
Rnd 13: [MC] *K2Tog, K 8 (10, 12), SSK, rep from * around – 50 (60, 70) sts.
Rnds 14 – 16: Work Rnds 1 – 3 of Ziggy Stripes pattern as established.
Rnd 17: [MC] *K2Tog, K 6 (8, 10), SSK, rep from * around – 40 (50, 60) sts.
Rnd 18: Work Rnd 1 of Ziggy Stripes pattern as established.
Rnd 19: *K2Tog, K 4 (6, 8), SSK, rep from * around – 30 (40, 50) sts.
Rnd 20: Work Rnd 3 of Ziggy Stripes pattern as established.

Child Size:
Go to Final Decrease.

Adult Size:
Next Rnd: [MC] *K2Tog, K4, SSK, rep from * around – 30 sts.
Next Rnd: Work Rnd 1 of Ziggy Stripes pattern as established.
Go to Final Decrease.

Large Adult Size:
Next Rnd: [MC] *K2Tog, K6, SSK, rep from * around – 40 sts.
Next Rnd: Work Rnd 1 of Ziggy Stripes pattern as established.
Next Rnd: [CC1] *K2Tog, K4, SSK, rep from * around – 30 sts.
Next Rnd: Work Rnd 3 of Ziggy Stripes pattern as established.
Go to Final Decrease.
Final Decrease: [MC] K2tog around – 15 sts.

Cut yarn, leaving 10-inch tail. Thread tail onto darning needle and run needle through remaining sts. Anchor tail with a stitch.

Finishing

Block on ironing board using wet cotton dishtowel to cover fabric and steam with a hot iron. DO NOT PRESS IRON DOWN ONTO FABRIC, just touch down lightly on wet towel to create steam. DO NOT BLOCK BRAID.

Weave ends into back of work with darning needle, leaving the tail at tip unwoven if adding a Fairy Pull or adding Twirlies. Top can be left plain or add a Twirlie or two, or crochet a Fairy Pull.

Twirlies:
Start with piece of yarn that is 4x the desired length of the finished cord (~24"). Fold in half. Grasp one end in each hand and begin twisting. Continue until, when relaxed (DON'T LET GO OF EITHER END), the cord begins to double back on itself. When ready, grab the center of the length (with your mouth if your are alone) and fold in half so the 2 ends are together (DON'T LET GO OF THE ENDS YET!) Let go of the center and the Twirlie forms. Knot the 2 ends together (don't let ends go until knotted). Run fingers along the length of the Twirlie to straighten out any kinks. Voila! Sew to the top of the hat with tail left at top of hat. Make another in another color if desired. Secure end to top of hat with darning needle and weave end into back of fabric.

Fairy Pull:
Using crochet hook use tail at top of hat and, beginning close to top of hat, chain 8 to 10 stitches then join chain back to top of hat. This creates the loop or pull. Secure end to top of hat with darning needle and weave end into back of fabric.

Color Harmony Cap

HONEY WINE BEANIE

by Erica Jackofsky

FINISHED MEASUREMENTS
18" finished head circumference x 7.5 (8)" length; hat is meant to be worn with 2-3" of negative ease.

YARN
Knit Picks Capra (85% Merino Wool, 15% Cashmere; 123 yards/50g):
Topaz 25576, 2 balls*.
If the entire hat is knit using the smaller needles you'll be able to finish with 1 ball (cuts it close on the yardage).

NEEDLES
US 6 (4mm) 16" circular needles and DPNs, or size to obtain gauge
US 7 (4.5mm) 16" circular needles and DPNs, or size to obtain gauge (optional, see pattern notes).

NOTIONS
Yarn Needle
1 Stitch Marker
Cable needle

GAUGE
28 sts and 17 rnds (one pattern repeat) equals 4.5" wide x 2.25" long, relaxed on smaller needles.
28 sts and 17 rnds (one pattern repeat) equals 4.75" wide x 2.5" long, relaxed on larger needles.

For pattern support, contact Erica@FiddleKnits.com

Honey Wine Beanie

Notes:
The cables used for this are widely spaced apart and allow the hat to stretch almost as much as it would if the pattern were a wide ribbing. This means that one finished size will fit a wide range of head sizes. Changing to the larger needle (optional) after the first 12 rnds lets the hat easily stretch to fit a mens 23" head circumference. For a tighter hat, or smaller heads, continue knitting with the smaller needles.

Working the pattern as written will give you a finished hat that is approximately 8" in length from the center of the crown to the cast on edge, provided you've matched the round gauge. If you opt to work the hat entirely on the smaller needles the finished hat will be approximately 7.5" in length. If you wish to alter the length slightly, either shorter or longer, you can easily do so by adding or subtracting a few even rounds at the end of each repeat. For example, for a hat that is a half inch shorter work rnds 1–15, skip rnds 16 and 17, begin the pattern again, and then skip rnd 16 and 17 the second time you get to them as well. This removes 4 rounds, which is approximately a half inch. Do the reverse to add a half in to the length, when you come to rnds 16 and 17 repeat them once more before proceeding.

Cable 2 over 2 Right
Slip 2 stitches to cable needle and hold back. Knit 2 stitches. Knit 2 stitches from cable needle.

Cable 2 over 2 Left
Slip 2 stitches to cable needle and hold front. Knit 2 stitches. Knit 2 stitches from cable needle.

Cable 2 over 1 Right
Slip 1 stitch to cable needle and hold back. Knit 2 stitches. Knit 1 stitch from cable needle.

Cable 2 over 1 Left
Slip 2 stitches to cable needle and hold front. Knit 1 stitch. Knit 2 stitches from cable needle.

Cable 2 over 1 Right Purl
Slip 1 stitch to cable needle and hold back. Knit 2 stitches. Purl 1 stitch from cable needle.

Cable 2 over 1 Left Purl
Slip 2 stitches to cable needle and hold front. Purl 1 stitch. Knit 2 stitches from cable needle.

Twist 2 Right
Slip 1 stitch to cable needle and hold back. Knit 1 stitch. Knit 1 stitch from cable needle.

Twist 2 Left
Slip 1 stitch to cable needle and hold front. Knit 1 stitch. Knit 1 stitch from cable needle.

Cable Pattern - One Pattern Repeat (in the round over 28 sts)
Rounds 1 and 2: K4, P2, K2, P2, K4, [P2, K2] 3 times, P2.
Round 3: K4, P2, K2, P2, K4, P2, cable 2 over 1 left purl, P1, K2, P1, cable 2 over 1 right purl, P2,
Round 4: K4, P2, K2, P2, K4, P3, k2, P1, K2, P1, K2, P3.
Round 5: K4, P2, K2, P2, K4, P3, cable 2 over 1 left purl, K2, cable 2 over 1 right purl, P3.
Round 6: K4, P2, K2, P2, K4, P4, K6, P4.
Round 7: Cable 2 over 2 left, P2, K2, P2, cable 2 over 2 right, P4, cable 2 over 1 left purl, cable 2 over 1 right purl, P4.
Round 8: K4, P2, K2, P2, K4, P5, K4, P5.
Round 9: K2, cable 2 over 2 left, K2, cable 2 over 2 right, K2, P5, cable 2 over 2 left, P5.
Round 10: K14, P5, K4, P5.
Round 11: K4, P1, twist 2 left, twist 2 right, P1, K4, P4, Cable 2 over 1 right, cable 2 over 1 left, P4.
Round 12: K4, P2, K2, P2, K4, P4, K6, P4.
Round 13: K4, P2, K2, P2, K4, P3, cable 2 over 1 right purl, K2, cable 2 over 1 left purl, P3.
Round 14: K4, P2, K2, P2, K4, P3, K2, P1, K2, P1, K2, P3.
Round 15: K4, P2, K2, P2, K4, P2, cable 2 over 1 right purl, P1, K2, P1, cable 2 over 1 left purl, P2.
Rounds 16 and 17: K4, P2, K2, P2, K4, [P2, K2] 3 times, P2.

DIRECTIONS

With smaller needles, cast on 112 sts.

Place marker and join for working in the rnd being careful not to twist sts.

Rnds 1-12: Work rnds 1–12 of cable pattern 4 times around circumference.

Optional: Change to larger needles. (This will produce a more relaxed fit on top.)

Rnds 13-17: Work rnds 13–17 of cable pattern 4 times around circumference.

Rnds 18-34: Work rnds 1–17 of cable pattern 4 times around circumference.

Rnds 35-39: Work rnds 1–5 of cable pattern 4 times around circumference.

Crown Decreases

Change to DPNs when necessary.
Rnd 40: *K4, P2, K2, P2, K4, P2, P2tog, K6, P2tog, P2; rep from * another 3 times – 104 sts.
Rnd 41: *Cable 2 over 2 left, P2 K2, P2, Cable 2 over 2 right, P3, cable 2 over 1 left purl, cable 2 over 1 right purl, P3; rep from * another 3 times.
Rnd 42: *K2tog, K2, P2, K2, P2, K2, SSK, P4, K4, P4; rep from * another 3 times – 96 sts.
Rnd 43: *K1, cable 2 over 2 left, K2, cable 2 over 2 right, K1, P4, cable 2 over 2 left, P4; rep from * another 3 times.
Rnd 44: *K2tog, K8, SSK, P4, K4, P4; rep from * another 3 times – 88 sts.
Rnd 45: *K2, P1, twist 2 left, twist 2 right, P1, K2, P2tog, P2, K4, P2, P2tog; rep from * another 3 times – 80 sts.
Rnd 46: *K2, P2, SSK, P2, K2, P3, K4, P3; rep from * another 3 times – 76 sts.
Rnd 47: *K2, P2, K1, P2, K2, P3, SSK, K2tog, P3; rep from * another 3 times – 68 sts.
Rnd 48: *K2, P2tog, K1, P2tog, K2, P3, P3; rep from * another 3 times – 60 sts.

Honey Wine Beanie

Rnd 49: *K2, P1, K1, P1, K2, P2tog, P1, K2, P1, P2tog; rep from * another 3 times – 52 sts.
Rnd 50: *K2, P3tog, K2, P2, K2, P2; rep from * another 3 times – 44 sts.
Rnd 51: *K2, P1, K2, P2tog, K2, P2tog; rep from * another 3 times – 36 sts.
Rnd 52: *K1, SK2P, K1, P1, K2, P1; rep from * another 3 times – 28 sts.
Rnd 53: *K3, P1, SKP, P1; rep from * another 3 times – 24 sts.
Rnd 54: *SK2P, P1, K1, P1; rep from * another 3 times – 16 sts.
Rnd 55: *K1, P1, SKP; rep from * another 3 times – 12 sts.

Cut yarn and pull through remaining 12 loops on needles to fasten top.

Finishing
Weave in ends. Lightly block if necessary. Take care not to over block. Hats must retain negative ease to fit properly.

Honey Wine Beanie

Honey Wine Beanie | 75

NUTKIN

by Erica Jackofsky

FINISHED MEASUREMENTS
19" relaxed forehead circumference x 7.75" long from center crown to cast on edge

YARN
Knit Picks Palette (100% Peruvian Highland Wool; 231 yards/50g): MC Clarity, 25548, 1 ball; CC Doe 24240 1 ball.

NEEDLES
US 2 (2.75mm) 16" circular needles, or size to obtain gauge
US 2 (3mm) 16" circular needles and DPNs, or size to obtain gauge

NOTIONS
Yarn Needle
Stitch Markers

GAUGE
32 sts and 37 rnds = 4" in 2 color ribbing on smaller needles.
30 sts and 34 rnds = 4" in stranded St st in the round on larger needles, lightly blocked.

For pattern support, contact Erica@FiddleKnits.com

Nutkin

Notes:

If you've hit gauge, the length of your hat will be 7.75" from the center crown to cast on edge. Achieving both stitch and round gauge is important for this design to turn out the stated size. Because you are following a non-repeating colorwork pattern there will be little opportunity to extend or shorten the length of the hat if your gauge is too small or large. The easiest way to add length is in the very beginning 2-color ribbing section. To decrease length it will be necessary to go down in needle sizes to shorten your round gauge.

Uneven floats (the strands on the WS of your work) will cause knitting to pucker and inhibit elasticity. For best colorwork results, wrap floats approximately every 2 to 4 sts.

Two Color Ribbing (in the round over an even number of sts)
Round 1: *Knit 1 with MC, purl 1 with CC; rep from * around.

Special Stitches
CDD - Central double decrease
Slip next two stitches together as if to knit. Knit 1 stitch. Pass two slipped stitches over the knit stitch. Two stitches decreased.

Skp — Slip, knit, pass (left slanting decrease)
Slip one stitch knitwise from left to right needle, knit one stitch, pass slipped stitch over stitch you just knit. One stitch decreased.

DIRECTIONS

With CC, cast on 152 sts. Place marker and join for working in the rnd being careful not to twist sts.

Attach MC. Do not cut CC.

Rounds 1-3: *K1 with MC, p1 with CC; rep from * to end of rnd.
Round 4: Knit with MC.
Rounds 5-50: Follow Squirrel Nutkin charted rows 5-50.

Crown Decreases

CC yarn may be cut (with a tail remaining for weaving in).

Change to DPNs when necessary.

Decreases are worked on every other rnd (odd numbered rnds).

Rounds 1 - 17: Work from Squirrel Nutkin crown decrease chart repeating stitches 1-19 a total of 8 times around circumference. 8 sts decreased on rnd 1, 16 sts decreased every other rnd.

Cut yarn and pull through rem 16 sts on needles. Fasten off.

Finishing

Weave in ends. Lightly block upper portion of hat to smooth out stranded knitting. Do not block ribbing.

Crown Chart

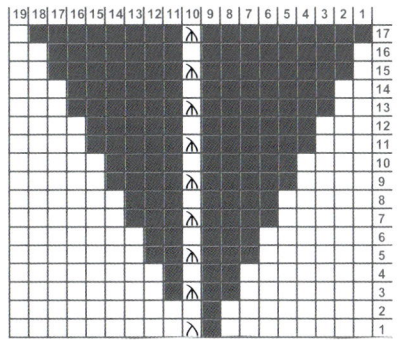

Legend:
- knit — knit stitch
- No Stitch — Placeholder - No stitch made.
- λ sl1 k psso — slip 1, knit 1, pass slipped st over k 1
- λ sl1 k2tog psso — slip 1, k2tog, pass slip st over k2tog

Legend:
- knit in MC
- knit in CC
- purl in CC

ROCK

by Fiona Hamilton-MacLaren

FINISHED MEASUREMENTS
19 (20.5, 22, 23.5, 25)" head circumference

YARN
Knit Picks Wool of the Andes Tweed (80% Peruvian Highland Wool, 20% Donegal Tweed; 110 yards/50g): 100g total, 10-20g each of five or six colors.
A Lost Lake H 25447
B Dill H 25456
C Brass Heather 25451
D Reindeer H 25962
E Rabbit H 25455

NEEDLES
US 7 (4.5mm) DPNs or two 24" circular needles for two circulars technique, or one 32" or longer circular needle for Magic Loop technique, or size to obtain gauge.

NOTIONS
Yarn Needle
Stitch Markers

GAUGE
20 sts and 28 rows = 4" in St st

For pattern support, contact contact@alittlebitsheepish.co.uk

Rock

Notes:
Knitted geekery always delights me. This hat is inspired by the profiles used by geologists to represent the layers of rock underground. Each strata is represented by a combination of yarn color and stitch pattern.

The arrangement of stitch patterns, colors, and stripe patterns can be varied by the knitter to create a unique hat. The hat is simple to make but gives you an opportunity to play with texture and color. Optional garter stitch earflaps can be worked for an extra cozy hat.

Each stripe uses a small amount of yarn, less than 1 ball of each color, so this project would be a great way to use up leftovers from other projects. You can vary the width of the stripes to suit the yarn you have available

Special Stitches
Stockinette (worked in the round)
All Rnds: K all sts

Garter stitch (worked in the round)
Rnd 1: K all sts
Rnd 2: P all sts
Rep Rnds 1 – 2 for pattern.

Seed stitch (worked in the round over an even number of sts)
Rnd 1: K all sts
Rnd 2: *K1, P1; rep from * to end of round
Rnd 3: *P1, K1; rep from * to end of round
Rep Rnds 2 – 3 for pattern.

Woven stitch (worked in the round over an even number of sts)
Rnd 1: K all sts
Rnd 2: *K1, sl1 wyif; rep from * to end of round
Rnd 3: K all sts
Rnd 4: *Sl1 wyif, K1; rep from * to end of round
Rep Rnds 1 – 4 for pattern.

Moss stitch (worked in the round over a multiple of 4 sts)
Rnd 1: K all sts
Rnd 2: *K2, P2; rep from * to end of round
Rnd 3: *K2, P2; rep from * to end of round
Rnd 4: *P2, K2; rep from * to end of round
Rnd 5: *P2, K2; rep from * to end of round
Rep Rnds 2 – 5 for pattern.

I-cord bind-off
Cast on 3 sts, slip onto left needle at start of round
K2, k2tog tbl, slip three stitches from right needle to left needle. Repeat around.

DIRECTIONS
Increases
Note: This section of the hat should be worked in either stockinette or garter stitch as these stitch types are not affected by the changing stitch count. If working this section in garter stitch, replace kfb with pfb (purl into front and back of next stitch). Sample shows the increase section worked in stockinette stitch in Color A. Change color and stitch pattern as desired to form stripes.

Cast on 8 sts. Either use the Emily Ocker cast on or leave a 6 inch tail for sewing up.

Rnd 1: Kfb around - 16 sts.
Rnd 2: *K1, kfb, pm; rep from * around - 24 sts, 8 markers placed.
Rnd 3: *K to 1 st before marker, kfb; rep from * around - 32 sts.

Repeat Rnd 3 5 (6, 7, 8, 9) times more - 72 (80, 88, 96, 104) sts.

On the final round, remove all markers except beginning-of-round marker.

Body of Hat
Work evenly for 46 (47, 48, 49, 50) rounds, or to desired length, in any combination and arrangement of the stitch patterns described above. Use one color of yarn for each stitch pattern.

Note: Sample shown is worked in the following sequence:
6 (6, 6, 6, 6) rnds garter stitch in Color B
4 (5, 6, 7, 8) rnds stockinette stitch in Color A
10 (10, 10, 10, 10) rnds garter stitch in Color B
8 (8, 8, 8, 8) rnds woven stitch in Color C
2 (2, 2, 2, 2) rnds stockinette stitch in Color A
7 (7, 7, 7, 7) rnds moss stitch in Color D
5 (5, 5, 5, 5) rnds seed stitch in Color E
4 (4, 4, 4, 4) rnds garter stitch in Color B

Ear flaps (optional)
Note: Work ear flaps in color used for garter stitch stripes. Sample shows ear flaps worked in Color B.

Rnd 1: k all sts
Rnd 2: p all sts

Begin short row shaping:
Row 1 (RS): k 25 (28, 31, 34, 37), pm, W&T
Row 2: k 17 (17, 19, 21, 23), W&T
Row 3: K to 1 st before last wrapped st, W&T

Rep Row 3 until 5 stitches remain unwrapped, ending on a WS row.

Row 4 (RS): K to marker, picking up and knitting wraps as you pass them, remove marker, k 40(42, 46, 50, 54), pm, wrap next stitch and turn work
Row 5: k 17(17, 19, 21, 23), W&T
Row 6: K to 1 st before last wrapped st, W&T

Rep Row 3 until 5 stitches remain unwrapped, ending on a WS row.

Row 7: K to marker picking up and knitting wraps as you pass them, remove marker. K to end of round.

Return to working in the round:

Next Rnd: P all sts around, picking up and knitting wraps as you pass them
Next Rnd: K all sts around

Bind off
Using a sixth color (or one of the previously used colors), bind off all stitches using an I-cord bind off. Sample shows i-cord bind-off worked in Color B.

Use yarn tail to sew ends of I-cord together.

Finishing
Weave in ends, wash and block.

Additional details, such as fossils, can be added using embroidery or needle felting if desired.

Rock

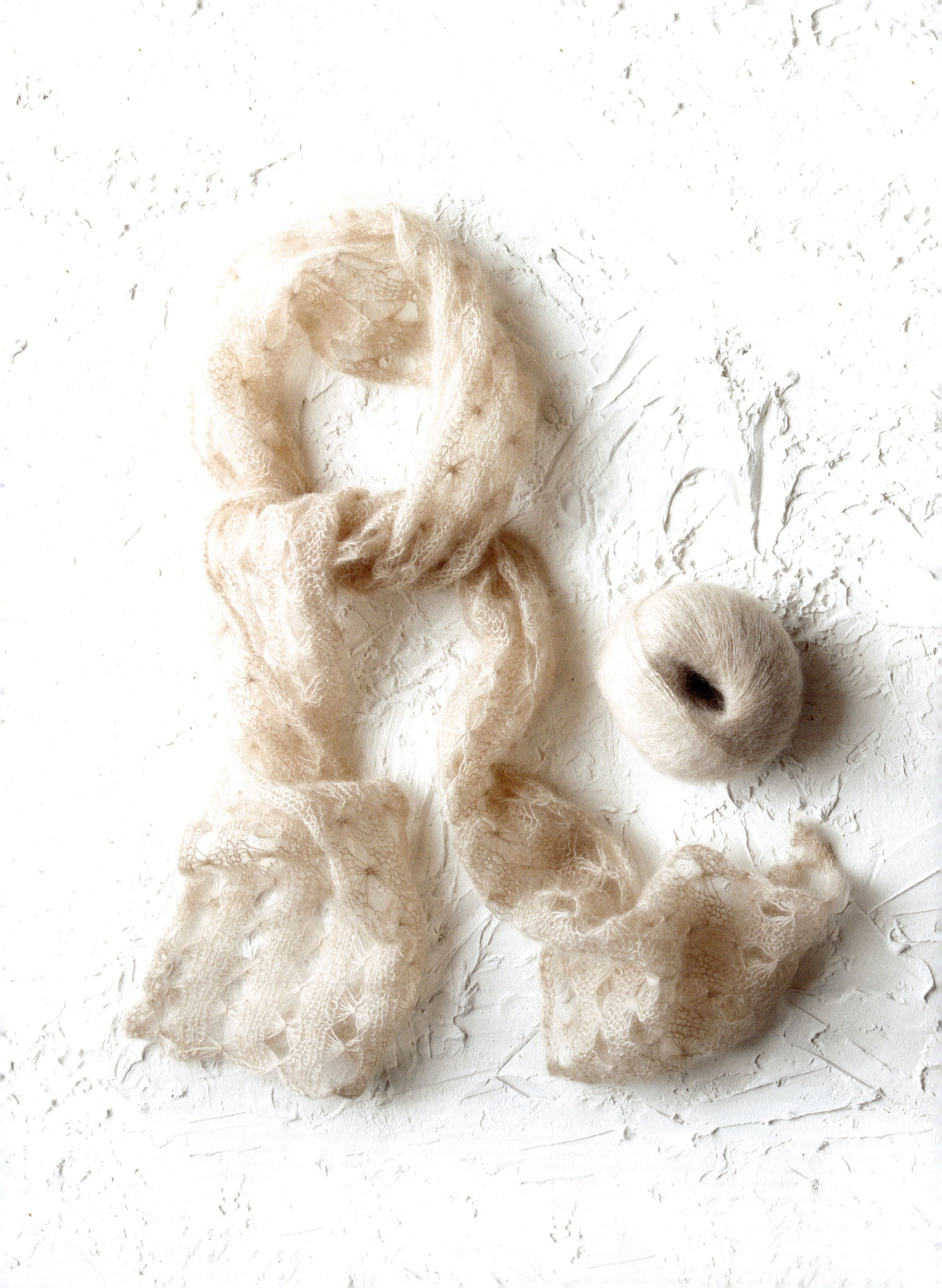

Neckwear

BUTTERFLY STITCH SCARF

by Alice Tang

FINISHED MEASUREMENTS.
8"wide x 65" long

YARN
Knit Picks Aloft (75% Super Kid Mohair, 25% Silk; 246 yards/25g): Oat 25756, 2 balls.

NEEDLES
US 5 (3.75mm) straight or circular needles, or size to obtain gauge

GAUGE
Each pattern repeat about 1 ¼" tall and 1 ½" wide, blocked.
Gauge is not critical.

For pattern support, contact tangram.knits@gmail.com

Butterfly Stitch Scarf

Notes:
YO2 (yarn over 2 times) - means wrap yarn around needle twice. The yo2 will be dropped in the next row.

DIRECTIONS
Using the long-tail CO (CO 3, make a space of about 1 ¼" with both ends of yarn) 6 times, ending with CO 3.

Row 1 (WS): (P3, YO2) 6 times, P3.
Row 2, 4, 6: (K3, drop YO2 from last row, YO2) 6 times, K3
Row 3, 5, 7: (P3, drop YO2s from last row, YO2) 6 times, P3
Row 8: K3 (YO, K1 from dropped YO2, all 7 strands except for 1st pattern repeat, which has 9 strands because of the CO, pass YO over this k stitch then slip to left needle and k again making a long loop, k, pass long loop over stitch, K2) 6 times.

Hint: When working row 8 of pat, tug on the dropped yarnovers to spread them to about 1" wide before knitting them together. Make sure the YO2 and long loops are even, manually adjust if needed.

Continue in pat for about 52 repeats or desired length ending with Row 7.

Row 8 of last pattern repeat: BO 2, (make long loop with last stitch, k1 from dropped YO2 and pass long loop over, slip this stitch back to left needle and k again making a long loop, BO 3) 6 times.

Finishing
Weave in ends, wash and block.

For a tutorial on this pattern, please check out http://www.tangramknits.com/Butterfly_Scarf with photos and additional help!

CIRRUNCINUS SHAWL

by Kate Schuyten

FINISHED MEASUREMENTS
64" (163 cm) long and 12" (30.5 cm) at deepest point in edging, after blocking. Note that exact measurements will vary slightly depending on gauge and how aggressively the shawl is block.

YARN.
Knit Picks Stroll Tonal Fingering (75% Superwash Merino, 25% Nylon; 462 yards/100g):
Springtime Tonal, 1 skein.

NEEDLES
US 5 (3.75mm) straight or circular needles
Or size to obtain gauge

NOTIONS
2 Stitch Markers
Yarn needle
Blocking pins

GAUGE
23 sts & 33 rows = 4"/10 cm in stockinette stitch, unblocked.
22 sts & 24 rows = 4"/10 cm in stockinette stitch, blocked.
Gauge is not crucial for this project, however differences in gauge will affect the final measurements of the shawl and amount of yarn used.

For pattern support, contact spiderkateknits@gmail.com

Cirruncinus Shawl

Notes:

Cirruncinus is a sideways knit shawl that starts with 14 stitches and increases up to 64 stitches before decreasing back down to the original 14 stitches. Markers are used in the pattern to separate out the stockinette body from the garter edge on one side and the lace edging on the other side. The body stitches are worked to the right of the lace edging. Increase and decrease rows are worked either every RS row for fast increases/decreases or on Rows 1, 5, 9, and 13 for slow increases/decreases.

It is important to work each section completely before moving on in the pattern with exception to the Straight Section. The Straight Section can be repeated more times than indicated in the pattern. If planning on doing more than 12 Cirruncinus Lace Stitch repeats, then make sure to leave approximately 25 grams (116 yds/106 m) of yarn to complete the final sections of the shawl (First & Second Decreasing and Finishing sections). If knitting to gauge, then you can safely knit one more repeat of the Cirruncinus Lace Stitch edging in the Straight Section.

Cirruncinus Lace Stitch (worked flat)
Row 1 (RS): K3, YO, K5, YO, K2tog, YO, K2. (14 sts)
Row 2 (WS): K2, P12. (14 sts)
Row 3: K4, SK2P, K2, YO, K2tog, YO, K2tog, K1. (12 sts)
Row 4: K2, P10. (12 sts)
Row 5: K3, SKP, K2, YO, K2tog, YO, K2tog, K1. (11 sts)
Row 6: K2, P9. (11 sts)
Row 7: K2, SKP, K2, YO, K2tog, YO, K2tog, K1. (10 sts)
Row 8: K2, P8. (10 sts)
Row 9: K1, SKP, K2, YO, K2tog, YO, K2tog, K1. (9 sts)
Row 10: K2, P7. (9 sts)
Row 11: SKP, K2, YO, K1, YO, K2tog, YO, K2. (10 sts)
Row 12: K2, P8. (10 sts)
Row 13: K3, YO, K3, YO, K2tog, YO, K2. (12 sts)
Row 14: K2, P10. (12 sts)

DIRECTIONS
Set-Up
CO 14 sts. Knit 2 rows.

First Increase Section
Row 1 (RS): K2, PM, M1, PM, work Row 1 of Cirruncinus Lace Stitch. (17 sts)
Row 2 (WS): Work Cirruncinus Lace Stitch, SM, Purl to marker, SM, K2. (17 sts)
Row 3: K2, SM, M1, Knit to marker, SM, work Cirruncinus Lace Stitch. (16 sts)
Row 4: Work Cirruncinus Lace Stitch, SM, Purl to marker, SM, K2. (16 sts)
Rows 5-56: Repeat Rows 3-4 26 more times ending with Row 14 of Cirruncinus Lace Stitch. (42 sts total: 2 edge sts, 28 sts in shawl body, 12 sts in Lace edge)

Note: Cirruncinus Lace Stitch is worked 4 full times at the completion of this section.

Second Increase Section
Row 1 (RS): K2, SM, M1, Knit to marker, SM, work Row 1 of Cirruncinus Lace Stitch. (45 sts)
Row 2 (WS): Work Cirruncinus Lace Stitch, SM, P to marker, SM, K2. (45 sts)
Row 3: K2, SM, Knit to marker, SM, work Cirruncinus Lace Stitch. (43 sts)
Row 4: Work Cirruncinus Lace Stitch, SM, Purl to marker, SM, K2. (43 sts)
Rows 5-12: Repeat Rows 1-4 2 more times. (43 sts)
Row 13-14: Repeat Rows 1-2 once. (46 sts)
Rows 15-28: Repeat Rows 1-14 once. (50 sts total)
Row 29-56: Repeat Rows 1-2 14 times, ending with Row 14 of Cirruncinus Lace Stitch. (64 sts total: 2 edge sts, 50 sts in shawl body, 12 sts in Lace edge)

Note: Cirruncinus Lace Stitch is worked 4 full times at the completion of this section.

Cirruncinus

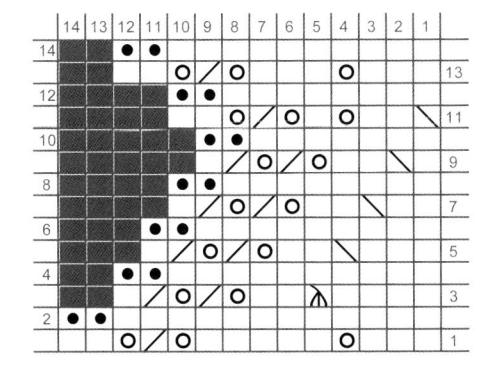

Legend:
- knit — RS: knit stitch / WS: purl stitch
- yo — Yarn Over
- k2tog — Knit two stitches together as one stitch
- purl — RS: purl stitch / WS: knit stitch
- sl1 k2tog psso — slip 1, k2tog, pass slip stitch over k2tog
- No Stitch — Placeholder - No stitch made.
- ssk — Slip one stitch as if to knit, Slip another stitch as if to knit. Insert left-hand needle into front of these 2 stitches and knit them together

Straight Section

Row 1 (RS): K2, SM, Knit to marker, SM, work Row 1 of Cirruncinus Lace Stitch.
Row 2 (WS): Work Cirruncinus Lace Stitch, SM, Purl to marker, SM, K2.
Rows 3-14: Repeat Rows 1-2 6 times, ending with Row 14 of Cirruncinus Lace Stitch.
Rows 15-168: Repeat Rows 1-14 11 times. (64 sts)

Note: Cirruncinus Lace Stitch is worked 12 full times at the completion of this section.

**See pattern notes on increasing the number of repeats in this section.

First Decrease Section

Row 1 (RS): K2, SM, K2tog, Knit to marker, SM, work Row 1 of Cirruncinus Lace Stitch. (65 sts)
Row 2 (WS): Work Cirruncinus Lace Stitch, SM, Purl to marker, SM, K2. (65 sts)
Rows 3-28: Repeat Rows 1-2 13 times. (50 sts)
Row 29: K2, SM, K2tog, Knit to marker, SM, work Row 1 of Cirruncinus Lace Stitch. (51 sts)
Row 30: Work Cirruncinus Lace Stitch, SM, Purl to marker, SM, K2. (51 sts)
Row 31: K2, SM, Knit to marker, SM, work Cirruncinus Lace Stitch. (49 sts)
Row 32: Work Cirruncinus Lace Stitch, SM, Purl to marker, SM, K2. (49 sts)
Rows 33-40: Repeat Rows 29-32 twice. (45 sts)
Rows 41-42: Repeat Rows 29-30 once. (46 sts total)
Row 43-56: Repeat Rows 29-42 once. (42 sts total: 2 edge sts, 28 sts in shawl body, 12 sts in Lace edge)

Note: Cirruncinus Lace Stitch is worked 4 full times at the completion of this section.

Second Decrease Section

Row 1 (RS): K2, SM, K2tog, Knit to marker, SM, work Row 1 of Cirruncinus Lace Stitch. (43 sts)
Row 2 (WS): Work Cirruncinus Lace Stitch, SM, Purl to marker, SM, K2. (43 sts)
Rows 3-52: Repeat Rows 1-2 25 more times. (13 sts)
Row 53: K2, SM, K2tog, SM, work Cirruncinus Lace Stitch. (13 sts)
Row 54: Work Cirruncinus Lace Stitch, SM, P1, remove marker, K2. (13 sts)
Row 55: K1, K2tog, SM, work Cirruncinus Lace Stitch. (14 sts)
Row 56: Work Cirruncinus Lace Stitch, remove marker, K2. (14 sts)

Cirruncinus Lace Stitch is worked 4 full times at the completion of this section.

Finishing

Knit 2 rows.

Loosely BO all sts knitwise.

Weave in ends and block to finished measurements.

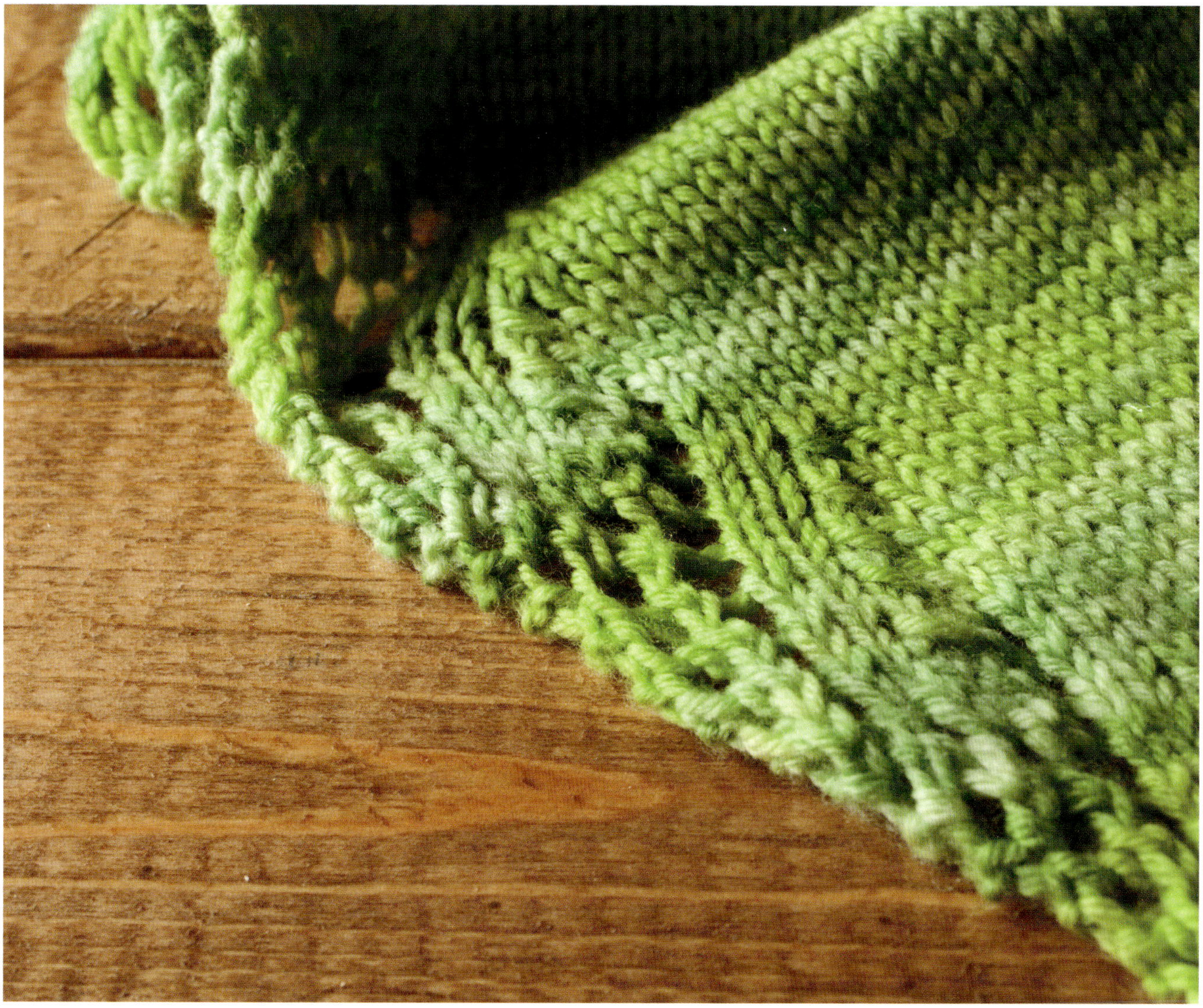

FERN SHAWLETTE

by Michele Lee Bernstein | PDXKnitterati

FINISHED MEASUREMENTS
17" back depth, 68" wide at top edge, blocked

YARN
Knit Picks Palette (100% Peruvian Highland Wool; 231 yards/50g): Ivy 23999, 2 balls

NEEDLES
US 5 (3.75mm) straight or circular needles, or size to obtain gauge
US 13/14 (0.90 mm) crochet hook for placing beads

NOTIONS
Yarn Needle
Stitch Markers
Size 6/0 seed beads, approximately 400, optional

GAUGE
20 sts and 38 rows = 4" in garter stitch, unblocked

For pattern support, contact pdxknitterati@comcast.net

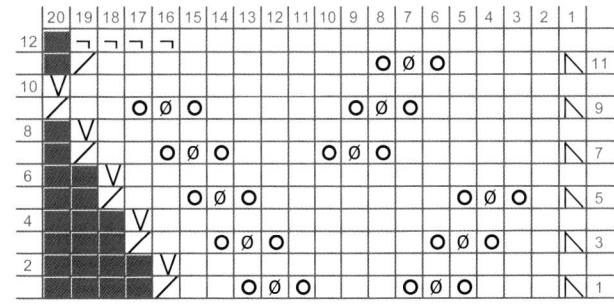

Fern Shawlette

Notes:
The Fern Lace Shawlette is worked flat, from side to side. It features a built in I-cord top edge, garter stitch body, and a Fern Lace edging. Gradual increases in the garter stitch section create a graceful crescent curve. Beads are optional, but they do add sparkle and weight for drape.

All slipped stitches are slipped purlwise, with yarn in front.

Techniques and Stitch Patterns
PB (Place bead): Place bead on crochet hook (you can pick up the bead from a shallow dish of beads with the crochet hook), hook stitch from LH needle and pull it through your bead, replace stitch onto LH needle and then knit it as usual. If you do not wish to use beads, simply knit the stitch.

SK2P: Slip 1 st knitwise, K2tog, PSSO. This creates a left leaning double decrease.

Elastic Bind Off
K2, *insert LH needle into fronts of these 2 sts from left to right and knit them off together through the back loops. One st bound off. K1; repeat from * as needed. This technique is used for all bind offs in this pattern.

I-Cord Edging
Row 1: K1, SL 1, K1
Row 2: SL 1, K1, SL 1

Fern Lace Edging (worked flat)
Row 1 (RS): SK2P, K3, YO, PB, YO, K3, YO, PB, YO, K2, K2TOG.
Row 2 & all even rows except 12: S1, P to end of edging.
Row 3: SK2P, K2, YO, PB, YO, K5, YO, PB, YO, K2, K2TOG.
Row 5: SK2P, K1, YO, PB, YO, K7, YO, PB, YO, K2, K2TOG.
Row 7: SK2P, K6, YO, PB, YO, K3, YO, PB, YO, K2, K2TOG.
Row 9: SK2P, K5, YO, PB, YO, K5, YO, PB, YO, K2, K2TOG.
Row 11: SK2P, K4, YO, PB, YO, K10, K2TOG.
Row 12: BO 4. One st remains on right needle. P to end of edging.

DIRECTIONS
CO 20 sts. P 1 row.

Setup rows
Establish sections using Fern Lace Setup Chart or written instructions here:
Row 1 (RS): K1, SL 1, K1, PM, K2, PM, SK2P, K6, YO, PB, YO, K5.
Rows 2, 4, 6: SL 1, P14, SM, K2, SM, SL 1, K1, SL 1.
Row 3: K1, SL 1, K1, SM, K2, SM, SK2P, K5, YO, PB, YO, K6.
Row 5: K1, SL 1, K1, SM, K2, SM, SK2P, K4, YO, PB, YO, K7.

These 6 rows establish the three sections of the shawlette: the 3 stitch I-cord edge, the Garter stitch body section, and the Fern Lace Edging.

Shawlette Body
Work established patterns as follows:
On RS rows, work I-cord edge over 3 sts, slip marker, K to next marker (increasing or decreasing as directed below), slip marker, work Fern Lace Edging to end.

On WS rows, work Fern Lace Edging, slip marker, K to next marker (increasing or decreasing as directed below), slip marker, work 3 stitch I-cord edge.

Work increases in Garter stitch section between markers as follows:

On Row 1 and every 4th following row (coinciding with Rows 1, 5, and 9 of Fern Lace Edging), K to 2 sts before marker, KFB in this st, K1. Continue until 17 repeats of Fern Lace Edging are complete—51 increases, 53 sts in the garter stitch section after 204 rows.

Work 12 rows even with no increases or decreases (one repeat of Fern Lace Edging) for center of shawlette.

Work decreases in garter stitch section as follows:

On Row 1 and every 4th following row (coinciding with Rows 1, 5, and 9 of Fern Lace Edging), K to 3 sts before marker, K2tog, K1. Continue until an additional 17 repeats of Fern Lace Edging are complete—51 decreases, 2 sts remain in the garter stitch section after 204 rows.

Finishing
BO all sts using Elastic Bind Off. Wet block to desired measurements. Weave in ends after blocking.

Legend:
- **Sk2p**: Sl 1 st, k2tog, pass slipped st over
- **knit**: RS: knit stitch, WS: purl stitch
- **purl**: RS: purl stitch, WS: knit stitch
- **Place Bead**: See instructions in pattern.
- **k2tog**: Knit two stitches tog as one stitch
- **No Stitch**: Placeholder - No stitch made.
- **slip**: Slip stitch as if to purl, holding yarn in front
- **Bind Off**
- **yo**: Yarn Over

IONA DOUBLE RUFFLE SCARF

by Quenna Lee

FINISHED MEASUREMENTS
50 (60)" long x 8.5" wide

YARN
Knit Picks Alpaca Cloud (100% Baby Alpaca; 440 yards/50g): Tidepool Heather 23502, 2 (2) hanks. 510 (610) yards.

NEEDLES
US 4 (3.5mm) straight or circular needles, or size to obtain gauge.
US 5 (3.75mm) straight or circular needles, or size to obtain gauge.

NOTIONS
Crochet hook for Provisional CO
Smooth Scrap yarn for Provisional CO
Stitch Markers
Yarn Needle

GAUGE
24 sts and 36 rows = 4" over Seed Stitch rib, blocked.
4.5" across and 3.75" high = one rep of Iona lace edging, blocked.

For pattern support, contact blissfulbyquenna@yahoo.com

Iona Double Ruffle Scarf

Notes:
Iona is knit horizontally with a center panel of Seed Stitch Rib. Stitches are increased before starting the lace edging. For the opposite edging, stitches are picked up from the provisional CO edge.

The first stitch of each row is slipped knitwise unless otherwise noted.

The first 3 and last 3 stitches of the scarf are worked in garter stitch.

Garter Stitch (worked flat)
Knit all sts.

Seed Stitch Rib (multiples of 2 +1, worked flat)
Row 1: Knit all sts.
Row 2: *[P1, K1], rep from * until 1 st left, P1.

Rep Rows 1-2 for pat.

Iona Lace Edging (multiples of 20 + 1 over 20 rows, worked flat)
Notes:
For odd rows, rep from *[] until 1 st rem, K1.
For Rows 2, 4, 6, 8, 18: Purl all sts.
For Rows 10, 12, 14, 16: Rep from *[].

Row 1: *[K3, YO, SSK, K3, K2TOG, YO, K1, YO, SSK, K3, K2TOG, YO, K2].
Row 3: *[K1, (YO, SSK, K1) 2 times, K2TOG, YO, K3, YO, SSK, (K1, K2TOG, YO) 2 times].
Row 5: *[K2, YO, SSK, K1, YO, K3TOG, YO, K5, YO, SK2P, YO, K1, K2TOG, YO, K1].
Row 7: *[K3, YO, SSK, K2TOG, YO, K7, YO, SSK, K2TOG, YO, K2].
Row 9: *[K4, K2TOG, K4, YO, K1, YO, K4, SSK, K3].
Row 10: P1, *[P2, SSP, P4, YO, P3, YO, P4, P2TOG, P3].
Row 11: *[K2, K2TOG, K4, YO, K5, YO, K4, SSK, K1].
Row 12: P1, *[SSP, P4, YO, P7, YO, P4, P2TOG, P1].
Rows 13-16: Rep Rows 9-12.
Row 17: *[K1, YO, SSK, K1, K2TOG, YO, K2, YO, K1, CDD, K1, YO, K2, YO, SSK, K1, K2TOG, YO].
Row 19: *[K2, YO, SK2P, YO, K3, YO, K1, CDD, K1, YO, K3, YO, K3TOG, YO, K1].
Row 20: Knit all sts.

Stretchy Bind-off
K1, *[YO, K1, sl 2 sts], rep from * to 1 st. Cut and pull yarn through.

DIRECTIONS
Center Panel
With larger needle and scrap yarn, Provisional CO 307 (367) sts. Work Seed Stitch Rib until piece measures 1" from CO, ending with a WS row. Switch to smaller needle.

Edging #1
Inc Row (RS): K3, PM, *[K2, KFB] rep from * to last 4 sts, K4. 407 (487) sts.
Setup Row: K3, PM, P21, PM, *[P20, PM], rep from * to last 3 sts, K3.
Rows 1-20: K3, work Iona Lace pat from chart or written instruction to last 3 sts, K3. There are 20 (24) horizontal rep of the Iona Lace pat.

While working the last row, remove markers. With larger needle, BO with Stretchy BO.

Edging #2
With WS facing, transfer 307 (367) sts from the scrap yarn to needle.
Set-up Row (WS): K3, purl to last 3 sts, K3.

Rep Edging #1 instructions, beg with Inc Row (RS).

Finishing
Weave in ends and block to finished measurements. To prevent center rib from stretching, block each lace edging separately. Pin center rib to measurements in a half circle (convex) to open up lace edging. Rep for the other side.

Iona Lace Edging Chart
Chart is read from the bottom up; right to left on odd rows (RS) and left to right on even rows (WS).

Legend:

- knit
  RS: knit stitch
  WS: purl stitch
- yo
  Yarn Over
- ssk
  RS: Slip two stitches knitwise one at a time onto right needle. Insert left-hand needle into front of these 2 stitches and knit them together
  WS: Slip two stitches knitwise one at a time onto right needle. Slip them back onto left needle and purl the two stitches together through back loops
- k2tog
  RS: Knit two stitches together as one stitch
  WS: Purl 2 stitches together
- k3tog
  Knit three stitches together as one
- sk2p
  slip 1, k2tog, pass slip stitch over k2tog
- CDD
  Slip 2 sts as if to K2tog, knit 1, pass slipped sts over

SILVRETTA CRESCENT SHAWL

by Simone Kereit

FINISHED MEASUREMENTS
65" across top edge, 20" back depth

YARN
Knit Picks Palette (100% Peruvian Highland Wool; 231 yards/50g): Spearmint 24253, 2 balls

NEEDLES
US 7 (4.5 mm) circular needles, 24" or longer

NOTIONS
Yarn Needle
Smooth waste yarn or stitch holder for provisional cast on
(optional) Stitch Markers

GAUGE
20 sts = 4" over stockinette stitch, blocked.
(Gauge for this project is approximate, but will affect yardage)

For pattern support, contact simone_k77@yahoo.com

Silvretta Crescent Shawl

Notes:
This crescent shaped shawl is worked top down in one piece, starting from a garter stitch tab at the top edge. Increases are worked along the outside edge on either side, and to keep it simple, the lace edging is only worked over the last 42 rows.

To maintain a uniform edge, always slip first stitch as if to purl, holding yarn in the back.

Special Stitches
Provisional Cast On (Figure-8 Loop method)
Make a slipknot and place it on your right hand needle. Holding a spare circular needle or waste yarn parallel to your working needle, bring the working yarn out in front of the spare needle, then loop it down and to the back, bringing it up and out in between the working needle and the spare circular needle, first st made. For each additional stitch, using a figure 8 motion, bring the yarn up and over the working needle from front to back and down behind, then bring it out to the front in between working needle and spare, loop it under the spare needle to the back and finish by bringing it out to the front, in between the needles.

Picot
Slip st from r needle back to l needle; knitting through both the slipped st and the next st together, M2 using knitted cast on; k1, [k1, psso] x 3
(first k1= first st on needle/stitch just made, second k1=the other stitch just made)

Knitted Cast on (M2)
Insert needle into stitch(es) as if to knit, pull up a loop but place on the left hand needle, repeat one more time = 2 sts made

Pine Tree Pattern
Row 1 (RS): Sl1, K2, Kfb, K1, [SSK, K2, YO, K1, YO, K2, K2tog, K1] x16, Kfb, K3.
Row 2 (and all following WS rows, up to Row 30): Sl1, K2, YO, P to last 3 sts, YO, K3.
Row 3: Sl1, K2, Kfb, K3, [SSK, K2, YO, K1, YO, K2, K2tog, K1] x16, K2, Kfb, K3.
Row 5: Sl1, K2, Kfb, K5, [SSK, K2, YO, K1, YO, K2, K2tog, K1] x16, K4, Kfb, K3.
Row 7: Sl1, K2, Kfb, K1, YO, K1, YO, K2, K2tog, K1, [SSK, K2, YO, K1, YO, K2, K2tog, K1] x16, SSK, K2, YO, K1, YO, K1, Kfb, K3.
Row 9: Sl1, K2, Kfb, [SSK, K2, YO, K1, YO, K2, K2tog, K1] x17, SSK, K2, YO, K1, YO, K2, K2tog, Kfb, K3.
Row 11: Sl1, K2, Kfb, K2, [SSK, K2, YO, K1, YO, K2, K2tog, K1] x18, K1, Kfb, K3.
Row 13: Sl1, K2, Kfb, K4, [YO, SSK, K2tog, YO, K1, YO, SSK, K2tog, YO, K1] x18, K3, Kfb, K3.
Row 15: Sl1, K2, Kfb, K2, K2tog, YO, K2, [K1, YO, SSK, K3, K2tog, YO, K2] x18, K1, YO, SSK, K2, Kfb, K3.
Row 17: Sl1, K2, Kfb, K3, K2tog, YO, K3, [K2, YO, SSK, K1, K2tog, YO, K3] x18, K2, YO, SSK, K3, Kfb, K3 – 205 sts.
Row 19: Sl1, K2, Kfb, [K3, YO, SK2P, YO, K4] x19, K3, YO, SK2P, YO, K3, Kfb, K3.
Row 21: Sl1, K2, Kfb, K2, [SSK, K2, YO, K1, YO, K2, K2tog, K1] x20, K1, Kfb, K3.
Row 23: Sl1, K2, Kfb, K4, [SSK, K2, YO, K1, YO, K2, K2tog, K1] x 20, K3, Kfb, K3.
Row 25: Sl1, K2, Kfb, K1, [YO, SSK, K2tog, YO, K1, YO, SSK, K2tog, YO, K1] x21, Kfb, K3
Row 27: Sl1, K2, Kfb, K4, K2tog, YO, K3,[YO, SSK, K3, K2tog, YO, K3] x20, YO, SSK, K4, Kfb, K3.
Row 29: Sl1, K2, Kfb, [K2, YO, SSK, K1, K2tog, YO, K2, YO, K1, YO] x21, K2, YO, SSK, K1, K2tog, YO, K2, Kfb, K3.
Row 30: Sl1, K2, YO, P to last 3 sts, YO, K3.

Border Pattern
Row 1 (RS): Sl1, K5, YO, K3, [YO, SK2P, YO, K1, K2tog, YO, K3, YO, SSK, K1] x21, YO, SK2P, YO, K3, YO, K6.
Row 2 (and all following WS rows, up to Row 10): Sl1, K2, P to last 3 sts, K3.
Row 3: Sl1, K3, K2tog, YO, K2, YO, SSK, K1, [YO, K1, YO, K1, K2tog, YO, K2, YO, K1, YO, K2, YO, SSK, K1] x21, YO, K1, YO, K1, K2tog, YO, K2, YO, SSK, K4.
Row 5: Sl1, K5, YO, SSK, K1, YO, [SSK, S2KPsso, K2tog, YO, K1, K2tog, YO, K3, YO, SSK, K1, YO] x21, SSK, S2KPsso, K2tog, YO, K1, K2tog, YO, K6.
Row 7: Sl1, K4, YO, K2, YO, SSK, K1, [YO, SK2Psso, YO, K1, K2tog, YO, K2, YO, K1, YO, K2, YO, SSK, K1] x21, YO, SK2Psso, YO, K1, K2tog, YO, K2, YO, K5.
Row 9: Sl1, K5, YO, SSK, K1, YO, SSSK, [YO, K1, YO, K3tog, YO, K1, K2tog, YO, K3, YO, SSK, K1, YO, SSSK] x21, YO, K1, YO, K3tog, YO, K1, K2tog, YO, K6.
Row 11: Sl1, K4, YO, K2, YO, SSK, K1, YO, [SSK, K1, K2tog, YO, K1, K2tog, YO, K2, YO, K1, YO, K2, YO, SSK, K1, YO] x21, SSK, K1, K2tog, YO, K1, K2tog, YO, K2, YO, K5.

DIRECTIONS
Start: Garter Tab
Cast on 3 sts using Figure-8 Loop method or provisional cast on of choice. Knit across all stitches, turn work and knit 19 more rows, always slipping first stitch. Turn work 90° and pick up 9 sts in the slipped edge stitches of your knit rows, pick up and knit the 3 temporary cast on stitches from the beginning = 15 sts on your needles.

Increase rows
Row 1 (WS): K3, YO, P9, YO, K3 – 17 sts.
Row 2 (RS): K3, Kfb, K to last 4 sts, Kfb, K3 – 19 sts.
Row 3 (WS): K3, YO, P to last 3 sts, YO, K3 – 21 sts.
Rep Rows 2 – 3, 37 more times, until you have 169 sts on the needle.

Proceed to work Lace Border.

Pine Tree Section
Work Rows 1 – 30 of the Pine Tree pattern following the chart or the written instructions. One additional repeat of the Pine Tree chart per side will be added on Rows 11 and 21.

Chart shows RS rows only. Work all WS rows as: Sl1, YO, P to last 3 sts, YO, K3.

You should have 273 sts after Row 30.

Border

Work Rows 1 – 11 of the Border pattern following the chart or the written instructions.

There are no more YO on the WS rows, and no Kfb on the RS.

Chart shows RS rows only. Work all WS rows as: Sl1, K2, P to last 3 sts, K3.

You should have 362 sts after Row 11.

Bind Off

Start row with Picot x 2 (but start first picot by working M2 into first st on needle, not slipping st from r needle back to l needle)

[P1, sl both sts on r needle back to left hand needle and p2tog] x10,
*[Picot Bind Off] x 3,
[P1, sl both sts on r needle back to left hand needle and p2tog] * x6

Rep from * to last 11 st,
end row with [P1, sl both sts on r needle back to left hand needle and p2tog] x10,
Picot x 2.

Cut yarn and pull end through.

Finishing

Weave in ends but don't cut threads until the end. Soak using wool wash, drain, and press out excess water, then fold in a towel and gently press on it to remove more water, then block using lace T-Pins and lace blocking wires. Pin shawl from the center out along the top increase edge in a slight crescent shape, then pin out center points of picot on bind off edge. Let dry completely before unpinning.

Silvretta Pine Tree

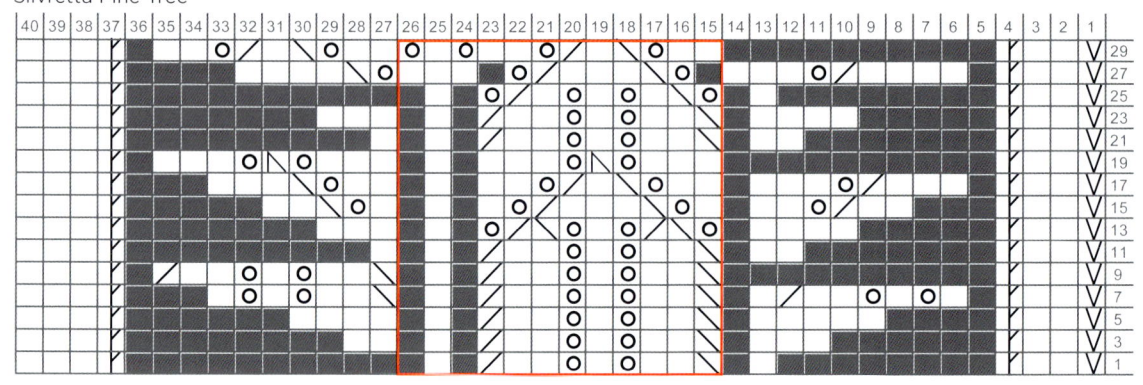

Silvretta Border

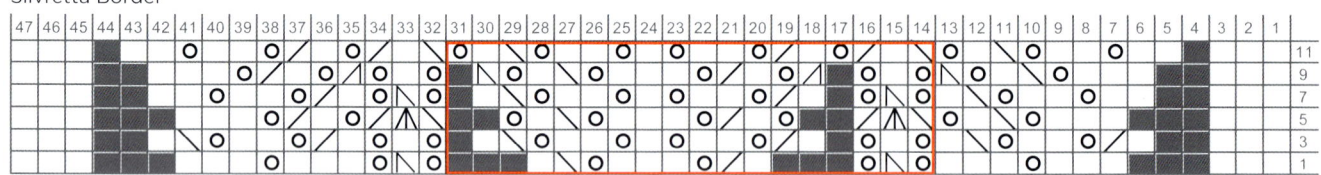

Legend:

- ☐ knit / knit stitch
- ■ No Stitch / Placeholder - No stitch made.
- O yo / Yarn Over
- ╱ k2tog / Knit two stitches together as one stitch
- ╲ ssk / Slip one stitch as if to knit, Slip another stitch as if to knit. Insert left-hand needle into front of these 2 stitches and knit them together
- ▲ Central Double Dec / Slip first and second stitches together as if to knit. Knit 1 stitch. Pass two slipped stitches over the knit stitch.
- ╲ sk2psso / Slip 1 st, knit the next 2 sts together, then pass slipped st over
- ╱ k3tog / Knit three stitches together as one
- V slip / Slip stitch as if to purl, holding yarn in back
- ϒ kfb / Knit into the front and back of the stitch

94 | Silvretta Crescent Shawl

Silvretta Crescent Shawl

Abbreviations

BO	bind off	K-wise	knitwise	P-wise	purlwise		tog tbl
cn	cable needle	LH	left hand	rep	repeat	SSSK	sl, sl, sl, k these 3 sts tog
CC	contrast color	M	marker	Rev St st	reverse stockinette stitch	St st	stockinette stitch
CDD	Centered double dec	M1	make one stitch	RH	right hand	sts	stitch(es)
CO	cast on	M1L	make one left-leaning stitch	rnd(s)	round(s)	TBL	through back loop
cont	continue	M1R	make one right-leaning stitch	RS	right side	TFL	through front loop
dec	decrease(es)			Sk	skip	tog	together
DPN(s)	double pointed needle(s)	MC	main color	Sk2p	sl 1, k2tog, pass slipped stitch over k2tog: 2 sts dec	W&T	wrap & turn (see specific instructions in pattern)
		P	purl				
EOR	every other row	P2tog	purl 2 sts together				
inc	increase	PM	place marker	SKP	sl, k, psso: 1 st dec	WE	work even
K	knit	PFB	purl into the front and back of stitch	SL	slip	WS	wrong side
K2tog	knit two sts together			SM	slip marker	WYIB	with yarn in back
		PSSO	pass slipped stitch over	SSK	sl, sl, k these 2 sts tog	WYIF	with yarn in front
KFB	knit into the front and back of stitch					YO	yarn over
		PU	pick up	SSP	sl, sl, p these 2 sts		